BUT YOU LOOK SO WELL!

A Story of Hope and Healing when Faced with Chronic Dis-ease

by
CAROL KRETSCHMER

Copyright © Carol Kretschmer 2023
Published by Healing from Within

Structural Edit by **Leeza Baric** at
https://LeezaBaric.com

Copy Edit and Proofread by **Poppy Solomon** at
https://poppyspagesediting.com

Cover and Interior Design by **Ina Kuehfuss** at
https://Inawonderworld.com

Disclaimer
All opinions expressed in the book are entirely the author's. Names have been changed for privacy reasons. The experiences and information within are shared freely from the heart. There is no intent to diagnose or treat your condition, rather to self-empower. Always consult your trusted health professional before embarking upon a new regime.

All rights reserved. No part of this book may be reproduced by any mechanical, photographic, or electronic process, or in the form of a phonographic recording: nor may it be stored in a retrieval system, transmitted, or otherwise be copied for public or private use other than for "fair use" as brief quotations embodied in articles and reviews without prior written permission of the author and/or publisher.

Cataloguing-in-Publication Data is on file at Legal Deposit State Library of South Australia and the National Library of Australia.

Ebook ISBN: 13: 978 0 645 7334 40
Tradepaper ISBN: 13: 978 0 645 7334 33

First Edition, April 2023

Dedicated to Love,

the most powerful positive force in the Universe,

and Hope, without which we are lost.

May you be forever blessed.

CONTENTS

ABOUT THE AUTHOR   IX

INTRODUCTION   XI

PART ONE
MY BACKGROUND AND STORY OF DIS-EASE

CHAPTER 1   3
The Burnt Potato Syndrome
(All Mums are Superheroes)

CHAPTER 2   11
Little Do We Know
(Stress is Real)

CHAPTER 3   19
The Wheels Fall Off
(How Could This Happen to Me?)

CHAPTER 4   29
Searching for Answers
(The Medical Merry-Go-Round)

CHAPTER 5   39
The Invisible Disease
(No One Understands, Not Even Me!)

PART TWO
HEALING FROM WITHIN – AN INTEGRATIVE APPROACH

CHAPTER 6   51
The MIND
(Our Thoughts Create Our Reality)

CHAPTER 7   63
The BODY
(Food, Nutrition and the Gut-Brain Connection)

CHAPTER 8   83
The SPIRIT
(Intuition and Psychic Senses)

PART THREE
NEW BEGINNINGS AND WELCOME SURPRISES

CHAPTER 9   105
Make Peace with Your Past
(Acceptance, Forgiveness and Gratitude)

CHAPTER 10   121
Angels and Miracles
(More Than Meets the Eye)

CHAPTER 11   135
Be Well with Me
(New Beginnings and Endless Possibilities)

PART FOUR
RESOURCES

TEN TOP TIPS FOR HEALTHY LIVING		153
Healthy Choice 1	QUIET THE MIND	155
Healthy Choice 2	BREATHE DEEPLY	157
Healthy Choice 3	DRINK SUFFICIENT WATER	159
Healthy Choice 4	REDUCE YOUR TOXIC LOAD	161
Healthy Choice 5	MANAGE YOUR STRESS	163
Healthy Choice 6	EAT REAL FOOD	166
Healthy Choice 7	HEAL YOUR GUT	168
Healthy Choice 8:	MOVE YOUR BODY	170
Healthy Choice 9	FORGIVE EVERYONE FOR EVERYTHING (including yourself)	172
Healthy Choice 10	HONOUR YOUR EMOTIONS	174
A FINAL NOTE FROM ME		176
FURTHER READING		178
ACKNOWLEDGEMENTS		182

ABOUT THE AUTHOR

CAROL KRETSCHMER is a physiotherapist, wellness educator, energy practitioner, angel intuitive, author and psychic channel. Her personal journey through chronic disease shifted her focus to a heart-centred approach. In addition to her formal qualifications, Carol now teaches diet and lifestyle choices, meditation and self-responsibility as the keys to life purpose and true vitality. Carol is a mother of two, grandmother of four, and lives with her husband, Ian on the coast of the beautiful Fleurieu Peninsula, (south of Adelaide) in South Australia.

To connect with Carol, please visit:

Website   https://carolshealing.com
Facebook   Carol's Healing from Within (https://www.facebook.com/profile.php?id=100063511253311)
Instagram (https://www.instagram.com/carolshealing/)
Email   carolaldinga@gmail.com

INTRODUCTION

Spoiler alert: this story has a happy ending! I hope that won't ruin the suspense for you, but it is in fact my 'happy ending' that has enabled and inspired me to write my story for you.

You, or someone you know, may be experiencing chronic disease or ill health of some kind. Perhaps countless 'experts' have told you 'there is no cure' and 'you just have to learn to live with it' or be medicated for life. Maybe you feel stuck with some aspect of your life or health journey and know that you need to find answers, move forward and not just cope, but live a vibrant life.

I was in the prime of my life when I suddenly got sick at forty-seven. I endured constant pain, hardship and at times sheer misery, which left me feeling helpless and lost for a very long time.

Although my story may be confronting for some, I want you to know that there is always hope in the face of adversity, and that we are more in control of our destiny than we may realise. As I recount the debilitating symptoms and the difficult years I experienced, I remind myself of all that I have gained and how much wiser, healthier and happier I feel as a result.

Most people appear to be suffering in some way. It may be from a diagnosed or recognised condition, or a more nebulous set of symptoms that seem to make no sense at all, but there is a common thread of dis-ease in the way it impacts our life. We have arrived at a state that is not aligned with our natural state of wellbeing and it doesn't feel good. We are not at ease, thus the hyphenation of dis-ease.

Everyone wants to be happy and healthy, but what are the fundamentals that create this lifestyle? Perhaps they are not taught in formal education. Even as a highly qualified primary health care provider, neither my common sense nor my extensive tertiary studies could prepare me for the up-close and personal experience of prolonged illness. I had to open my eyes to a much bigger picture and a truly holistic approach to wellness. Luckily, in time, I found all of that and more deep within me.

If you are caught up in any sort of pain, turmoil, grief or disease, please know that I have been there too! You may be stuck 'in it' now, unable to see a clear path ahead, but I am thrilled you have picked up this book so I can help you find your way out.

I am writing this account of my own life experience to give you back your HOPE, but also to supply you with a host of practical tools. Compassion, from all I have been through, has kept me learning and growing so that I now have the means to short circuit your own journey.

With good judgment and perspective you will be able to make the changes you need in your life for optimal health. Even as I write this book, which I trust will be of assistance to others, I know that the experience is for me as well. It's another step forward in my healing and personal evolution. It has been a quite cathartic process already.

I started to write this book long before Covid-19 was on our radar. At times, while negotiating the massive global changes that it has brought, I began to doubt if I would ever complete the task. My manuscript stalled repeatedly, taking a back seat as I tackled other requirements of life. Had I been too slow and 'missed the boat'?

An epiphany gave me the impetus to move it along again. I felt excitement about all the people it may help. Restoring hope in an uncertain world was my very reason for embarking upon this labour of love in the first place.

The epiphany was this: There has been great suffering in our world. Many souls have lost their equilibrium. My book will be needed more than ever.

I was a 'late bloomer' in some respects, slow to explore a broader approach to health. However, it now appears that I had to take this long and difficult path in order to learn so much. We can certainly accumulate wisdom from overcoming adversity and living through difficult journeys. But that does not necessarily have to be the case for you. There is no need for you to reinvent the wheel. You are more than welcome to piggy-back on my 'success', with the lessons and skills that I have already learned.

It is my great pleasure to share with you my experiences, insights, skills and simple strategies. Many of these I already knew but they were flying under the radar and not being heeded! Deep down we know what we have to do; sometimes we just need some encouragement and support along the way.

I am aware, of course, that we are all different. Each of you will have your own path to tread in order to discover what works best for you. There is no 'one size fits all' recipe or even a manual for navigating life. You must discover your own unique way of healing. However, let the path I have forged and the tools I have gathered serve as an example and give you hope. Perhaps you will piece some of them together and start to turn your own life in a more positive direction.

Allow your body to find its way back to its natural state of good health, and welcome joy back into your life. Take my hand and I will show you how.

***

PART ONE

MY BACKGROUND AND STORY OF DIS-EASE

CHAPTER 1

The Burnt Potato Syndrome (All Mums are Superheroes)

'LIFE TEACHES YOU HOW TO LIVE IT, IF YOU LIVE LONG ENOUGH.'
- TONY BENNETT

I am told I have a high IQ, but guess what? That doesn't necessarily make me smart!

I was previously unaware of the importance of tapping into one's own intuition; this is where true wisdom actually comes from. Sometimes it seems the smartest thing we can do is 'unlearn' what we have been taught. We are often running outdated programs or engaging old beliefs that are no longer helpful. Perhaps when we let go of logic, magic can happen.

Intuition, when coupled with intellect, will bring forth wisdom. This equation rings true for me: INTELLIGENCE + INTUITION = WISDOM. It has been a long and winding road on my journey from chronic disease to wellness and wisdom.

In order to make sense of where I am now, let me take you back in time.

I was born and raised in sunny South Australia, and shared a room with my older sister Sandra in a two-storey house my dad built. I was a sporty kid; a lean redhead who preferred to be outside shooting hoops to inside practising piano. Apart from a few tumbles down the stairs, I had a fairly uneventful childhood in a loving home, although Dad was prone to drinking too much and Mum was often sick. I learned from an early age, it seems, to put the needs of others ahead of my own.

I was a healthy child and an eager student. I enjoyed university and made some very good friends there. At the age of twenty-one, after four years of tertiary studies, I proudly graduated in my chosen field. At last, I was a fully qualified physiotherapist. I set about working in various wards of a large public hospital in my hometown. My husband, Ian, and I were also married that year, and we settled into our first family home. We didn't have many material things, but we were happy there and didn't mind at all that our ironing board had to double as a dining table. It was part of the adventure!

Before long, I was promoted to the position of Chief Physiotherapist at a smaller community hospital. I was young and relatively inexperienced, but excited that they placed their trust in me. I welcomed the opportunity to supervise staff and learn new administrative skills. Proudly I recall my first pay cheque buying us a washing machine.

My husband and I both worked hard, and he took on a second, part-time position. This allowed us to save in preparation for the extensive overseas travel that was his dream. I was always quite happy as a 'homebody' (a Cancerian trait, I'm told) and was greatly enjoying the challenges of my new career, but Ian was very keen for us to broaden our horizons. So, a few years later, we found tenants for our little town house and embarked upon twelve months of 'leave without pay'. We set off on our adventure to explore the big wide world.

It was a truly wonderful experience, and although I had been the one dragging my heels about going, I soon became enchanted and enthralled by the vast history and amazing scenery. We explored much of the United Kingdom and continental Europe by campervan, bussed across the United States, skied in Canadian snow fields at Christmas and warmed ourselves in Hawaii and Fiji before our first look around lovely New Zealand. We landed back home in Adelaide almost a year later, with a bucketload of new experiences under our belts and no regrets.

On our return to Australia, we were very fit and suntanned, and very broke. But we had the security of jobs to come back to and would always be glad that we did that amazing year of travel together, and while we were so young. Especially so when it became evident that we had brought home an extra special little souvenir. Yes, you guessed it: a blood test on my first day back at work confirmed that I did not have a tummy bug. I was, in fact, a little bit pregnant! We had made a beautiful little bundle of joy in Fiji.

We busily set about buying a larger home, doubling our mortgage and halving our income. I continued to work until close to full term and all went very well. In October we were blessed with the safe arrival of a perfect, bouncing, baby boy, Matthew.

Six weeks later, I embarked upon a career shift that led, in time, to a thriving private practice in the field of women's health. Initially I taught four childbirth classes each week (in the evenings while Baby was with his dad). This led to patients requesting treatment for their pregnancy ailments, as well as consultations while in hospital – for instruction on how to recover their stamina and muscle strength. I was even blessed to be present at several births, when couples invited me along as an extra support person. I look back now at how amazing it was that they included me in such an intimate event. At one birth, I gloved up and actually 'caught' a baby as he arrived into the world; the cheeky doctor tricked me into thinking I was just standing by to observe.

Before long, I was visiting all the maternity hospitals in town, with regular referrals from many of the obstetric specialists. I set up a clinical room at home and worked part-time from there at first, but eventually moved into more purposeful premises in a prominent central location.

We greeted Harry the golden retriever puppy into our home when our son was one, and in time we were blessed with a sweet baby girl. Sally arrived in June, two-and-a-half years after her brother. Our family unit was complete.

I loved my work, but I can now see I allowed it to rule my life. As my upbringing and 'people pleaser' personality dictated, I was afraid to say 'no' to anyone, and I ended up working ridiculous hours each week. I also adored my children and relished quality time with them, avidly pursuing their extra-curricular interests. My husband was wonderful at stepping into the breach and keeping things running smoothly at home. He didn't seem to mind that I was always leaving him with 'to do' lists!

I was trying to keep many balls in the air, with a total lack of regard for myself. I rarely gave myself permission to stop or slow down. While juggling work, home, family, relationships and financial aspects of my life, where was I in the equation?

We escaped on some camping holidays to trek in the bush and sit around campfires, and I adored that. In fact, I discovered a great love for our Australian Outback that still endures. These adventures replenished me, and they were wonderful family bonding times. I wish we had done more of this 'getting back to basics'. Stresses were adding up and when I look back, those red flags seem so obvious now.

As my physiotherapy practice grew, I didn't realise it was already taking a toll on my health. Isn't hindsight a wonderful thing? I loved the clinical work, but I felt completely out of my depth with practical business duties such as employing staff and tendering contracts. In the public hospital sector, I had felt like a welcome part of a multidisciplinary team, and I enjoyed the spirit of cooperation. In private practice, I soon learned that I was in a very competitive environment, and I was never entirely comfortable with that. I always loved sharing what I had learned – with patients, colleagues and other disciplines; the nurses I lectured, for example. Although I was well compensated, financial reward has never been a big motivator for me. It distressed me that everyone appeared to be disconnected and that others were only looking after themselves and holding on tightly to their own vested interests. Ironically, I was to learn the hard way that we must always put our own needs first and that everyone around us will benefit when we do.

At this stage of my life, I didn't even know how to nurture my own fundamental needs – and I held the erroneous belief that it would have been selfish to ever put myself first! This was probably because of the way I was raised, as well as the line of thinking that was contained in generations of DNA before me. I had not fallen into a 'caring' profession by mistake. Looking after others felt so natural. I had always done this because I loved to feel needed.

Isn't it fascinating that as women, our 'seed' was made in our mother's ovaries while she was forming within our grandmother? This mind-blowing fact explains a lot about how our behaviours are passed down through the ancestral line. As author Mitch Albom says, 'Behind all your stories is always your mother's story, because hers is where yours begins.'

A lovely doctor who visited the same hospitals as me offered some prophetic advice one day: 'You know, you don't always have to wear your briefs on the outside of your tights.' I think he was aware (more than me it seems), that I always went above and beyond, and extended myself to give everything my all. Hence the 'Wonder Woman' reference. My expectations of myself were indeed very high, but so were my genuine care for others and my desire to better their lives. Most of this has not changed, but now I listen to my body as well and strive to keep more balance in my life.

A patient once told me of an adage that I had not heard before but have always remembered. It was about the 'burnt potato syndrome'. She said, 'It's just what mothers do.' When we are dishing up the Sunday roast, we tend to give ourselves the burnt potato! In other words, we often put the needs of others before our own and are even inclined to put ourselves last in most situations. My mother denied herself many personal luxuries so that my sister and I could have new uniforms or afford sporting memberships, excursions and such like. She was a great seamstress and made us many outfits too. And I certainly saw Mum swallow her words repeatedly, trying to keep the peace rather than value her own opinion. Without my knowledge, I had taken on this trait from generations past. I was playing out this pattern without realising what it was, or that there might be undesirable consequences.

It occurs to me now that important life skills are often absent from our education curriculum. We are often not trained in self-awareness at home or at school. It is imperative that we learn how to identify our own specific needs so we can address and nurture them. I am always thrilled when I hear of schools that include meditation and mindfulness training, for these are pearls of wisdom that will continue to serve us well.

At the peak of my career, a good friend of my mother asked me to research something for her, and I have never forgotten her response when I promptly gave her what she wanted to know. 'When you want something done right, you can always rely on a busy woman!' Acknowledging my own 'burnt potato syndrome' and the wise words of my mother's friend were both light bulb moments for me. However, taking action was another matter, and for quite some time I continued to make my own needs a low priority. In fact, I'm not sure I even knew what my needs were then, let alone that they were important. That is, until a health crisis led me to examine my life under a microscope.

CHAPTER 2

Little Do We Know!
(Stress is Real)

'EVERYTHING WILL BE OK IN THE END. IF IT'S NOT OK, IT'S NOT THE END.' **- JOHN LENNON**

Stress is the number one epidemic of our civilisation, and is broadly recognised as an associated factor in all illness. Unaddressed stress is now a common component of 'underlying cause' in a vast array of mental and physical ailments.

Looking back at the timeline of my life events, it is easy to see that we packed a lot into our days, and I didn't allow myself the downtime that may have achieved more balance. As the wonderful Eckhart Tolle rightly points out, 'In today's rush, we all think too much, seek too much, want too much, and forget about the joy of just being.' I don't think I even knew what stress was then, or how I could have managed it better. In hindsight, many factors may have precipitated my downfall.

In 1998, after eighteen years in our first true family home, which our children were born and raised in, we embarked upon another phase in our lives and made a major move to a leafy suburb on the other side of town. During this time, our eldest was also studying for his final year at high school (which most students and parents find to be stressful). We loved our new home and neighbourhood, and it was much closer to our kids' secondary school, but moving house is always a big deal.

To make matters worse, we soon discovered that this lovely bungalow was kind of 'falling down'. We had unwittingly bought the worst house in the best street. Serious structural underpinning and revamping soon had to be undertaken, and it felt like we were living on a building site. I will always remember the incongruous image of the workers shovelling up rubble from my bedroom carpet! Still, we all survived and it was to my great relief that Matthew and Sally's hard work paid off and they received good grades, despite all the chaos and distractions at home. However, helping everyone through these times was often exhausting.

Unfortunately, the move had taken a physical toll on my husband. Ian has always had troublesome hip joints due to a joint malformation condition he was born with (Epiphyseal Dysplasia), and he had already undergone many minor surgeries in search of some temporary relief. But now he was in serious pain, unable to sleep or function well at all. We both knew the dreaded day had arrived where Ian would have to surrender to a major surgery: bilateral total hip replacements. He was only forty-four. Over three weeks spanning Christmas and New Year, he had both hip joints replaced with prosthetic implants, in surgeries that were only a week apart.

It was a terribly challenging time for us all (primarily Ian, of course), and with extra staff holding the fort at my physio practice, I pushed myself to the limit to be at the hospital for long hours. I may have been acting out of a need to control, as my personality dictated back then, but I was also totally dismayed by the absence of compassion and cohesive care in that relatively new, purpose-built orthopaedic hospital. I felt that I couldn't leave his side, because I had no faith in the staff to take care of him. But who was taking care of me?

To make things worse, my hubby got very sick from the narcotic pain relief, so it proved to be a tenuous recovery. They gave him large doses of this prescription medication in hospital, which created a chemically induced hepatitis (liver inflammation). Not at all ideal! By the way, it was actually me who picked this up. It was holiday season so doctors were not visiting as often as usual, and the nursing staff didn't seem to notice Ian's lethargy, poor appetite or grey complexion. I asked them to cease his pain drugs and he started to improve. Then we waited another day for a physician to visit (with a very big fee) only to confirm my assessment. What a frustrating and inefficient system. I am concerned for those who have no loved ones to advocate for them.

I clearly remember crying big tears of joy and relief when I first heard from the doctor that they completed his surgery. I mistakenly thought his brand-new hip joints would herald the end of his lifelong troubles. Only wishful thinking, I'm afraid. How naive of me!

Isn't it interesting that as humans we are wired for survival, and that is the role of the nervous system? And yet decades of societal constructs have led us to believe that only doctors have the answers (surgery and pharmaceuticals). It's a loop that many don't escape, but it is my updated belief that it is always good to step out of our comfort zone to question and challenge the status quo. Especially now that we are aware many illnesses are metabolic; directly related to our diet and lifestyle choices.

Our teenagers were pretty self-sufficient while their dad was in hospital, but I worried that I could not be there for them very much, and to top things off, our son was brutally assaulted that New Year's Eve. I was home alone when at 3am I received the call that all parents dread from the hospital emergency room. It was a random, unprovoked attack that had split his head open. Fortunately, they were able to patch him up with sutures and send him home, and he appeared to recover well. I think Matthew coped much better than I did. Strangely enough, he sunk a hole in one when playing golf the following week. It was an extraordinary time of highs and lows.

Eighteen months later, in the year 2000, I had the opportunity to move my physiotherapy practice to a suburb closer to home. Business volume had outgrown the premises I was previously in, and by joining forces with two complementary practitioners to share the rental costs, we were able to secure a prime spot. There was a lot to do and much negotiation and planning, but it was an exciting time.

My husband had, by this time, left his secure survey drafting job and was working as our practice manager. Not all couples could work together I'm sure, but Ian and I were a great team in all aspects of life and it felt pretty natural to us. But out of the blue, Ian's right hip started to cause him excruciating pain, and before long he was back in hospital; the joint replacement surgery had to be revised due to scar tissue getting caught in the joint. The poor man had three hip replacements in less than two years.

I had to recruit whatever help I could muster to make that move. Matthew and Sally offered their support as well as much practical assistance, and some kind friends supplied a trailer and extra muscle power. But I relied on Ian so much that I found it very hard to push through without him. Even then, the Universe was encouraging me to stand on my own two feet and acknowledge my innate strength. I just didn't realise it.

2000 was also the year our daughter studied Year 12. She did very well, but there were plenty of emotional ups and downs. Sally tended to lack self-confidence, and became very stressed by exams (as so many kids do!). I felt her pain, and didn't always know how to help her. Of course as parents we can absorb our children's stress without even knowing it. We want to make things right for them, but it can't always be like that. I know this now.

Emotional stress is insidious but can impact our health on all levels. I mentioned before that I loved being a physiotherapist, but in private practice, where I had found my niche, it was competitive and even confrontational at times (and I had never coped well with confrontation). It soon became evident that the other therapists and I were not always on the same page. Our vision and priorities for the centre differed a great deal, which did not engender the spirit of cooperation I had longed for.

In 2001, my hay fever allergy was out of control. The sneezes and drippy nose were affecting my ability to work, so I sought medical advice (the only path I knew back then). After many tests and consults, the doctors suggested a course of desensitising injections. Skin prick tests had shown my main allergens to be South Australian grasses, olive trees and a common weed called plantain.

My metaphysical reference books tell me that the mental and emotional aspects of hay fever include a suppression of feelings. Too much stress and worry. No time for yourself. Sadly, I didn't know much at all about the immune system or other aspects of health, so off I trotted to be injected with a cocktail of the things I was most allergic to. Once a week for four weeks, then once every month for the next three years, or at least that was the plan. Every injection caused a very painful reaction in my arm, so severe that I was unable to work for the rest of that day. They started to break it down into two half doses, given in two different spots, but it was still terrible. My body was trying to tell me something; it seems so obvious now!

I continued to work hard, and my practice was very busy. We won a contract for work with a big private hospital. I employed more staff, and although it was financially rewarding, I certainly did not enjoy the politics and red tape. Where was all this heading?

When I fell ill early in 2003, our son was preparing to leave home and move interstate to be with a girl he had not known for very long. Matthew was twenty-two and I was forty-seven, so he had of course been central to most of my adult life. On a logical level, I had great trust in the upstanding level-headed young man he had become, and I knew I had to let him 'fly'. I was happy and excited for him and his adventure. But I also knew that I would miss him (and our close-knit family life) terribly, and I certainly could not have predicted the profound effect that this milestone event would have on me as a mother. After he left, there were many days that I would secretly go into his room to sit on his bed, hug his pillow and cry. I have never admitted this to anyone until now. It makes me feel a little foolish, but I was in deep pain.

Looking back, I understand that my immune system had been thrown into chaos by the course of 'vaccinations' I was undertaking for the hay fever. I was also under more emotional stress that I wasn't managing well, in both my work and family.

Of course, we are now all well aware just how radically stress can further deplete and even paralyse the immune system.

In another irony of the Universe, I have since discovered that plantain weed (one of my allergens) is not only edible but has also been used for centuries in traditional medicine as it contains compounds that may reduce inflammation and improve digestion. It certainly did not offer my body those benefits when injected, however. Quite the contrary!

CHAPTER 3

The Wheels Fall Off! (How Could This Happen to Me?)

'DIFFICULT ROADS OFTEN LEAD TO BEAUTIFUL DESTINATIONS. THE BEST IS YET TO COME.' **- ZIG ZIGLAR**

So exactly when, where, how and why did I get so sick? Well, the last weekend in January of 2003 proved to be a fateful time for me. My husband and I were camping with friends and kayaking on the beautiful Murray River on an extraordinarily hot (47 degrees Celsius) long weekend. Being a true water baby, I was loving it. Water sports were my joy. As an adult, I had always wind surfed, water skied, body boarded and so on, but on this occasion, something was not quite right.

I was unaware but my body was under attack. My nose was streaming, my eyes were sore, and it felt like the worst hay fever I had ever experienced – only amplified ten times. We were out to dinner at the local country pub that night and I was not having a good time. I had to borrow tissues and antihistamines from our friends just to get me through. I guessed it was some sort of crazy allergy and was sure I would be OK in the morning.

But this illness caught me by surprise with its sudden onset and ferocity. The pathogen I had picked up managed to incubate very fast in the hot and humid conditions. We were sleeping in a small dome tent and the heat was oppressive. At night I had to drape a wet sarong over my bare body in order to get any rest.

Normally, I'm sure my immune system would have had my back. Under siege, it would recognise the threat and come to my rescue with a 'No way Jose, we've got this!' But in this case, instead of responding to protect me, it was like the struggling steam engine battling uphill and crying out, 'I think I can, I think I can,' but then realising, 'Oh no. I actually can't right now.'

We were back home after a few days and I don't recall exactly how long this lasted, but as days and weeks went by, whatever it was continued to change, morphing into a significant tummy upset that, at the time, I probably put down to a bad luck bout of gastro. Of course, it would eventually prove to all be related. Before long, I realised I also had a constant headache and lethargy that wouldn't let up. I battled on, continuing to work and expecting to get better – because that's what always happens, isn't it?

A couple of months later, I decided I had better see my local doctor. She had no idea what was going on with me other than a 'virus', so she took some bloods and sent me on my way. My sister and I then took our mother up to Queensland's Gold Coast for a few days to celebrate Mum's seventieth birthday. My son had just moved there, so I was very keen to catch up with him as well.

We stayed in a lovely apartment, walked on the beach, sat in the spa and did lots of fun activities, but I felt pretty terrible the whole time. My head ached constantly and my energy was depleted. Every day it felt like I was getting a bad flu. I would lie down with a wet cloth over my sore eyes at every opportunity.

Before I headed home, I took a phone call from my general practitioner. My results were in and she absolutely floored me when she suggested I take time off work – several months, in fact! My head was spinning. How could I stop working? I was the principal physiotherapist in a busy private practice. My patients and my staff relied on me, and my husband worked for me too. Surely this couldn't be happening!

My doctor warned me that if I kept working, I ran a great risk of developing Chronic Fatigue Syndrome. 'What the heck is that?' I thought. Was this what they called the ongoing low energy levels and extreme tiredness I was already experiencing? Of course I now know it is much, much more – a complex multi-system syndrome that is poorly named and has historically been misunderstood and even much maligned. So home I went, and I tried to work out how the wheels would keep turning without me.

I'm still not sure what it was about my blood results that alerted my doctor. All she told me was that I had tested positive for Glandular Fever (Epstein-Barr virus) and I needed to rest. I was lucky that Ian, as the practice manager, was running the practical, administrative, side of things at work. We restructured the diary and juggled the staffing as best we could in order to still accommodate our patients and the doctors who referred them.

It took another couple of weeks to be able to phase myself out, and then I tried to allow myself to lie low. Ian and the physiotherapists who worked for me stepped up and tried to leave me in peace, but on my end it was not easy to switch off.

I was unwell and bemused and I truly didn't know how to rest. This situation was very foreign to me. I did my best to not worry. I got hold of some good library books, and throughout that winter I sat in my rocking chair in front of our open fireplace. I loved the cosy heat from the glowing logs and started to even relish this downtime, despite how unwell I was. I still fully expected that I would recover, although nothing seemed to be changing in terms of my symptoms – that remained very prevalent. It probably didn't help my cause that I was stoic by nature. I'm also a redhead, and it has been proven that we have a higher pain threshold. Redheads even require higher dosage of anaesthetic compared to most people. It is literally harder to get us to rest!

After a few months, the staffing roster at the practice required me to return to work. One of the physios was expecting a baby and needed to take leave. I am now acutely aware of the need to set personal boundaries, but at the time I had not yet learned to say 'no', so back to the practice I went! I worked at reduced hours, but it was still extremely difficult. I struggled to get through my consultations – especially the more physically demanding ones.

This was the work I loved, but I was needing to lie down between patients just to recover enough to continue! My body could not provide the energy to sustain even the simplest routine. I also needed to take regular anti-inflammatory pills that sometimes only took the edge off the headache. I cringe now when I think of the additional damage these pills must have done to my digestive tract, and how the gut-brain connection was only adding to my symptoms!

I knew that this pattern was not sustainable, but I didn't know what else to do, so I battled on in this way for another couple of years. Rest hadn't worked, and I wasn't given any other treatment strategies. I started to worry that there was no solution and I might never recover.

My husband was under a lot of pressure. I had no energy or quality time for him or for poor Sally, who was still living at home with us. I knew she didn't understand what I was going through. I felt guilty as a mother, but I had no way of explaining it even to myself!

I realised that I should extricate myself from the business. Every aspect of it simply felt too hard. I had been unable to increase my work hours, but the practice was branded in my name and I had become quite well known. The therapists who worked with me were all excellent, but the majority of the patients and referring specialists still asked for me. We needed to establish a new paradigm for our small business.

One night, during my now disturbed sleep, I sat up in bed and made a decision. I just 'knew' that I needed to stop working and find a way to get well. So, I met with a couple of friends who were able to advise about rebranding the practice, and we created an updated business name, fresh logo and appointment cards. A whole new look and feel with broader appeal.

I felt inspired to move out of the city too, so we set about trying to sell the business and look for a new home. We explored a new location on the beautiful Fleurieu Peninsula, in the McLaren Vale wine-growing region south of Adelaide.

I felt very drawn to the south. We didn't know anybody there and had previously only done day trips to the wineries. However, we started to search the area for our next home. I didn't know what I wanted, just that I needed to be somewhere quieter. My husband only stipulated a preference for a house with a view.

We looked at many properties amongst the vineyards but found nothing that excited us until we drove home via the coast one day. A near-new two-storey house sat one street back from the beach, with a balcony that had glimpses of the ocean and horizon. The kitchen and main living area were upstairs amongst the trees and the birds, which also appealed to us a great deal. There was a lot I liked about it. Only my dad discouraged us, saying that this house was 'upside-down' which wouldn't be popular when we came to re-sell. He didn't like that the kitchen and living areas were upstairs and the bedrooms downstairs.

The price, however, was a bit steep for us. We had to be practical, as our income had already dropped and was about to take another dramatic hit. We put this lovely home to the back of our minds and soldiered on, considering building in order to get what we wanted, until several months later.

While in Queensland visiting our son, we got a call from the real estate agent to tell us the house was still on the market and the vendors had dropped their price for a quick sale. We didn't rush back to look at it, but when we finally did, all I can say is that it felt like we were walking into our home.

We had never owned a modern house before, and this complete sea change started to excite us. On careful inspection we realised that this was a quality-built home, and very well appointed. Solid timber floors, granite benchtops and all in a style that we would have chosen. There really was nothing that we didn't like about it, and we could now not think of any reason that we shouldn't go ahead. When we asked some close friends to appraise it with a critical eye, they responded, 'If you don't buy it, we will!'

And so our greatest leap of faith began. We placed our near-city character bungalow on the market, and it proved to be a good investment for us. We moved to our lovely little 'upside-down' house on the coast, 'mortgage free' for the first time in thirty years.

As for my physiotherapy practice, we were aware it would be a difficult business to sell. In my heart I knew that for my wellbeing I might just have to close the doors, and I was coming to terms with that. Surprisingly, at the eleventh hour, one of the delightful therapists, Tessa, who had worked with me for many years, decided she would take it over. She was understandably reluctant at first, as her two boys were still quite young, but she also knew this was a very good business with a reliable referral base and a lovely clientele. We were very happy for her to purchase it for a nominal fee and keep my beloved business going. My husband also offered to stay on part-time as her employee, to run her diary and 'keep the books'. That was seventeen years ago, and she is still there and going well.

There was one rather big hiccup at the start of that transition, though. I was exhausted, emotionally and physically wrung out, and very ready to have some quiet time. But Tessa sustained a very serious wound from broken glass, which required microsurgery to reattach the tendons of her thumb. A nasty injury for anyone, but potentially career-ending for a physio.

I felt great compassion for her predicament, but I cried that night for both of us at the same time. How was I going to dig deep once more and keep the business running while she recuperated? It felt like the Universe was playing a cruel trick. But with my amazing man at my side to drive me to and from the practice (now forty kilometres each way), handle all the tricky stuff, and restructure the diary so I could take sufficient breaks, I was enabled to cope, and we all survived for another few months. Luckily Ian's hips were doing quite well by this time, and I am so glad to say that Tessa got expert care and made a full recovery with the best possible outcome.

Looking back, I don't know how I managed to get through all of that, but I was very determined to change my lifestyle. My circumstance had been intolerable and certainly not working to my advantage or aiding my recovery. I now thank myself for listening to my intuition and following the inspiration that came, even though I did not understand just how important this was at the time.

In the meantime, our son had moved to the United Kingdom with his girlfriend to live and work in London for a year (which became four years), and our daughter moved into a flat near the city to avoid long commutes to work. We were to be empty nesters, and life would never be the same. I was being given space to focus on myself for perhaps the first time in my fifty years of life.

So, you can probably see how, on that sunny camping weekend, my life suddenly changed forever. The illness I contracted seemed to have no end! Most days, for a long time, I would have to choose between preparing a meal or taking a shower, as I would rarely have enough energy for more than one task. Unfortunately, pain, fear and hopelessness go hand-in-hand and breed despair. Sufferers live with a degree of chronic stress that most healthy people can't begin to comprehend. That was my life for many years. By this time, I was a shadow of myself and could barely function. I mostly endured in secrecy, as my somewhat 'invisible illness' went largely unseen by others.

Below is a 'List of Current Symptoms' that I collated in June 2008, more than five years after the onset of my illness. This was now two-and-a-half years after leaving work and moving to our new home in the south. I started to keep a diary of my symptoms in order to monitor and make sense of them. Sometimes, I mapped them hourly to see if any clues arose. Focusing upon how poorly I was feeling was probably somewhat counterproductive, but I didn't know what else to do!

* Constant **HEADACHE**, pressure and throbbing; varies only in intensity. It is the last thing I am aware of before sleep and the first thing I feel on waking.

* **BRAIN FOG**, ongoing. Like thinking through mud! Makes even the simplest tasks difficult.

* Limited **ENERGY** reserves, needing frequent rests, lying down or sitting with my head back.

* Post exertion **FATIGUE**, both mental and physical, therefore an extremely limited activity level. If I feel well enough to walk on the beach or ride my bike, I 'crash' for another day or two.

* **SLEEP** dysfunction. I still require a lot of sleep (ten to twelve hours per night) and do not feel benefit on waking, that is, not refreshed. Afternoon naps are common as well. Some nights it is very hard to get to sleep, or I wake many times.

* Sore **EYES**, a feature from the beginning. Worse when feeling more tired, but persistent.

* **NAUSEA**. I never know if this is because of the severe pain I'm in, or is a gastrointestinal symptom. I also have an irritable bowel habit.

* **PAIN** in the back, especially thoracic area (mid-back) if I try to stand for a while. Frequent 'tired ache', therefore needing to sit or lie down.

* General **MALAISE**. I feel unwell all the time, like endlessly getting the flu.

* **SENSITIVITY** to light and noise, always. Often needing to close my eyes. Great difficulty concentrating on a conversation if there is background noise like a radio.

* Impaired **MEMORY**, especially short-term. Difficulty concentrating and often slow with finding the right words.

* Recurrently sore **THROAT**, especially when at my worst.

* Intolerance of **TEMPERATURE** changes and can't handle extremes – plus night sweats and occasional hot flushes.

* Heart **PALPITATIONS** and dizziness. These were quite severe and more frequent earlier on but can still occur.

Even now, I still find this list hard to look back on, as it evokes such unpleasant memories. But I was determined to make some sense of it all.

CHAPTER 4

Searching for Answers (The Medical Merry-Go-Round)

'IF YOU CHANGE THE WAY YOU LOOK AT THINGS, THE THINGS YOU LOOK AT CHANGE.' - **DR WAYNE DYER**

When I first got sick, I was quite slow to grasp the idea of alternative therapies and healing. After all, I was a science girl! Science was my background and my strength (or so I thought). I studied physiotherapy at a university level, which included anatomy, physiology, histology and physics. You get the picture.

I had also been immersed in the 'medical model' for my entire life and working career. My parents had always sought and followed a doctor's advice for any ills that cropped up, and they each had a very long list of medical and surgical events in their lifetime. I had no idea about natural health, and in fact was initially rather closed off to the idea. My focus was quite narrow. That is, until my wellbeing was in question, as is often the case.

Off I went to consult with every medical specialist known to man, searching for elusive answers. My doctors suspected I had an autoimmune disease (which occurs when the body's immune system attacks healthy cells), but no one seemed to know the root cause. My Income Protection insurance policy required me to see my general practitioner often, and it soon became clear that she did not know at all what to do with me. She just kept issuing referral after referral.

Over time, I saw a very long list of medical specialists, including multiple neurologists, rheumatologists, endocrinologists, gynaecologists, immunologists and psychologists. The doctors were always said to be the most highly regarded experts in their field, and even as a private patient, I often waited months for an appointment. As I looked forward with anticipation, I tried to be hopeful about what they could offer me, only to have my hopes severely dashed time after time.

I am a seeker of truth and have never been a quitter, so I kept on hopefully attending all of these consultations, month after month, year after year. But I was appalled with the poor level of understanding, on both professional and empathetic levels. It was clear that all anyone in the field of conventional medicine could suggest was, at best, dulling my symptoms (but at what cost?) and certainly not addressing their underlying cause. They only offered me Band-Aids or stop-gap measures that were not solution-based, and they were in no way alleviating my disease. I can now cite numerous cases of people who have had (and continue to have) similar experiences where they feel their problems are being dismissed – but at the time I felt very alone.

One of the failures of conventional medicine, when it comes to autoimmune or other systemic metabolic diseases, is that nobody is looking at the broad scope of the immune system. For gut issues, doctors send us to a gastroenterologist. For thyroid, an endocrinologist, and so on. They are all looking at the individual organ that has been affected, but there is no cohesive or unified approach to diagnose or treat the overall condition. As a physiotherapist, I had been blatantly aware of this, but now as the 'patient' it was immensely frustrating and disheartening.

I have heard that if you have one autoimmune disease, you are three times more likely to get another. But who is capturing these statistics, and for what purpose? Chronic illness develops over time, so the 'quick fix' model of mainstream medicine is unlikely to work. Unfortunately we humans are often prone to look for instant gratification these days, in many aspects of our lives. 'Autoimmune' is a medical label that is often given when the cause is unclear. Even in the middle of our global immune crisis, we are fixated on 'finding cures'. Surely prevention is always a far better approach than cure. When solving problems, we must address the cause and 'dig at the roots instead of just hacking at the leaves'.

A heart-breaking turning point in my healing was when I visited a well-known rheumatologist, who I was told had been doing research studies on Chronic Fatigue patients. After waiting four months to see him, I described the debilitating headache that was my most troubling symptom, and explained that I wanted to know why I had it. He was less than helpful, offering no clues at all about underlying cause. When I politely refused his offer of a prescription for stronger painkillers, he had the audacity to tell me, 'You are obviously not desperate enough!' I looked at him in shock and disbelief. Then I stood and left his office with as much dignity as I could muster. Such arrogance, and a total lack of compassion. How dare he presume to walk in my shoes?

I rushed to the car and fell into a heap. I was outraged, deflated and crushed, and cried all the way home. Ian drove of course, but the depth of my devastation left me unable to speak to him on our long car trip. I just wanted to curl up in a ball and hide! I was sad for Ian too. I knew he was angry with the doctor and felt helpless about my situation. Once home, he ran a warm bath for me, and I tried to talk with him about how I was feeling. If this was the best health care available, we could not see that there was any hope for me. It was time to head in another direction.

An early clue about the link between my symptoms and food strangely appeared in relation to my heart palpitations. These would be frequent and usually short, but they escalated to a point where one day (in 2005) my daughter and niece witnessed a prolonged attack and insisted on taking me to hospital. The barrage of tests that followed in the emergency department (and referrals on to cardiac specialists) showed that it was a malfunction in the electrical impulses to my heart. Their recommendation was to undergo a minor heart surgery (Gulp! Is there even such a thing?) where they would use a wire to cauterise some nerves that supply my heart. I really didn't like the sound of that but rescheduled for a review down the track.

As luck (or divine intervention) would have it, one Friday evening soon after, I finished work late and made an easy dinner of toasted sandwiches. Not long after eating, the palpitations fired off badly again. Something in me recognised that it was at least partly because of the high-carbohydrate meal. I had eaten four slices of bread in one sitting, which was unusual for me. So, I started to experiment with cutting back, and I felt much better.

The palpitations disappeared and my review appointment was cancelled (by me). I can only imagine what the reaction of my heart specialist would have been if I'd tried to convince him that

I had solved my 'problem' by not eating bread! But I still didn't really know the best way to eat, and I muddled on for a long time until a helpful plan emerged.

In January 2007, I took myself to a somewhat 'alternative' doctor who was a General Practitioner (GP) but dealt mostly with hormones. Because of my age, and the lack of answers elsewhere, I started to question if this was all about approaching menopause. I found him to be a very eccentric chap with atypical methods, but four years into my illness, he turned out to be the first doctor who actually helped me.

My blood tests showed him I was indeed peri-menopausal, but my hormone levels were satisfactory. He was, however, very alarmed at the level of inflammation in my body. In four years, no one had mentioned this before (or even tested for it, as far as I knew!). He recommended a couple of supplements and told me in no uncertain terms that I needed to eliminate quite a few foods. I will never forget his exact words: 'If you keep eating the way you are, you will die!'

I didn't think my diet was too bad, and I was also aware that his approach may have been an overly dramatic, but the scare tactics worked! And I was definitely shocked into following his guidelines. From the moment I left his office, with the little list of foods to avoid (handwritten on notepaper advertising Viagra, might I add), I completely avoided the following: pasta, potato, pumpkin, rice, breads and cereals, sugar in any form, caffeine and alcohol. It was a strict proposal, but I did not find it to be difficult.

I was so glad to have a concrete plan of action that I could follow at last, and guess what? For the first time in four years, my headache changed. It was still there, but it seemed less intense, and my head was clearer. The brain fog was lifting! No one had ever before suggested a link between foods and my symptoms, but there was clearly something to this. The change in my diet was making a difference, and there was a glimmer of hope again. I was committed to continue, and to learn whatever else I could. I started to take back responsibility for my own health, and gradually took over the reins.

My eventual diagnosis of Chronic Fatigue Syndrome (CFS), and more specifically Myalgic Encephalomyelitis (ME), was arrived at by a process of elimination. My GP had given me a brochure to read about CFS/ME long before, and I certainly ticked all the boxes of the symptoms that were listed. But no one had definitively given my illness a label. It felt like this was the name given to a complex chronic illness when doctors didn't really know what was going on!

What I had was an autoimmune disease that attacks the brain and the central nervous system. It falls under the umbrella of Fibromyalgia. Finally, knowing 'what it was' felt both validating and soul destroying, as there were no apparent solutions for my condition.

Soon after, in March 2007, I found a live presentation called 'Myalgic Encephalomyelitis / Chronic Fatigue Syndrome: Breaking news from around the world', which was surprisingly being hosted in my hometown. There, I learned a great deal more. A panel of medical experts detailed the latest research and treatment protocols. I discovered that CFS/ME is classified as a neuro-immune disease. They spoke of this illness as complex, multi-system and multi-organ, often being described as 'low grade heart disease'. It was the first time I had heard that, but it started to make sense of my level of disability.

These experts also outlined how the pain and fatigue are from 'central' origins (the central nervous system), and that there was no evidence of any pharmacological products helping, including antidepressants (which had been repeatedly offered to me, but I had continued to resist). They talked about food intolerances like gluten, fructose and dairy. These were new and fascinating concepts to me. They even discussed gene mutations, that is, altered gene signatures that might be inherited or even secondary to the CFS disease.

It all got me starting to think outside the square as they talked about nutritional supplements and integrative doctors who have a more holistic approach – and more promising results. I felt uplifted as I left the seminar. I became guardedly optimistic about the prospect of regaining my health, or at least the real possibility of improving my quality of life – all of which had been so elusive.

Someone on the panel mentioned a doctor in the UK who was having some success with these cases, so I tried to follow her advice that I found online. I also discovered a local, experienced integrative doctor who saw lots of Chronic Fatigue cases. He ordered blood tests that had not been considered before, plus a brain scan and hair tissue mineral analysis. I was highly embarrassed to be sending away a sample of my pubic hair, as my scalp hair had been treated with hair dye that might skew the results! But this lovely man proved to be the first doctor who helped me make sense of what was occurring in my body.

One of the new blood tests returned positive to a Rickettsia bacteria called spotted fever, which in my case was a strain carried by ticks that live on reptiles in the region of our Riverland where I had been camping. When I suddenly got sick, this had been the trigger for my illness!

The CT scan of my brain showed many sclerotic lesions like the ones seen in Multiple Sclerosis (MS), and erosion of the myelin sheaths, which protect neurons. I consulted with a 'top' neurologist who reviewed these scans and told me, 'It might be MS, we can't be sure. Come back when you have more symptoms.' Not a satisfactory approach!

My new integrative doctor was able to explain, however, that this is a common picture seen in many cases of CFS/ME. The erosion was due to the levels of inflammation in my brain. No wonder I had constant head pain. He also found that I had a gene variant called the methylenetetrahydrofolatereductase (MTHFR) mutation, an often overlooked factor in CFS. This can cause nutritional deficiencies that are directly involved in the body's energy production at a cellular level. This was another associated factor that had been mentioned at the seminar. I still found it hard to accept all of this, but at least the pieces of the puzzle were falling into place.

These new insights also prompted me to go on a trip to the UK, where I could have blood tests called a 'Mitochondrial Function Profile', which were not yet available in Australia. After all, my son had been living and working in London for a couple of years and I was very keen to visit him there. I didn't know how my body would stand up to it, but I was determined to find a way, and I was excited. I quite enjoyed the planning, a happy and much more positive focus to occupy some of my time. At this point, I realised this illness had completely hijacked my life and robbed me of joy.

Despite all the trepidation, our travels turned out to be the most wonderful experience. It was great for my self-confidence and brilliant to have some unbridled joy of living to focus on again.

Interestingly, I felt relatively well while I was there and off all medication! We did our best to make it as painless as possible, with restful stopovers in Hong Kong in both directions, including several days to regroup on the way back. Once home, the travel took another temporary toll on my health, but it was totally worth it. Celebrating Matthew's birthday in Paris with him and his lovely girlfriend was such a heart-warming experience, and a nurturing memory that will forever make me smile.

I would also like to acknowledge just how difficult it can be to keep searching for answers when you are 'running on empty'. Luckily (or not?), I am stubborn. I am seeker of truth, and very persistent by nature – but how hard it is to have to drive this process ourselves! And even more difficult, I'm sure, for those who don't have the basic understanding of the body that my studies and career have brought me, or a supportive partner like I have been blessed with.

My Mitochondrial Function Profile came back from the UK showing a very low score of only 25/100. The mitochondria are the powerhouses of the cells. This poor result meant that I was like a four-cylinder car running on only one working cylinder, which certainly summed up how I felt. I was indeed using up energy at a greater rate than my body could replenish it.

The test also showed that I had cell-free DNA, a biomarker of cellular stress and inflammatory processes. I received these results with very mixed feelings. On one hand, they verified in black and white why I felt as bad as I did. I was certainly not crazy or making this up. On the other hand, it showed that my body was still pretty 'broken', and it was now almost five years since my illness took hold. No one seemed to have any idea how to fix it. I felt validated yet deflated, but I tried to remain hopeful.

The UK doctor who interpreted the tests was an integrative practitioner with a special interest in my type of illness, and I followed her suggested protocol of medications and supplements for quite a long time with no perceived benefit, and patches of negative side effects as well. The South Australian doctor I had found, who also had experience with autoimmune conditions like mine, did his best to customise treatment protocols to suit me. I really appreciated his efforts, but we still seemed to get nowhere fast.

This was all leading me to a point where I had to assume full responsibility for turning things around. The roller coaster continued, and there was a surprising rock-bottom point looming just around the corner.

CHAPTER 5

The Invisible Disease
(No One Understands, Not Even Me!)

'YOU CAN'T GO BACK AND CHANGE THE BEGINNING, BUT YOU CAN START FROM WHERE YOU ARE AND CHANGE THE ENDING.'
- CS LEWIS

As a clinical physiotherapist with many contacts 'in the system', I once believed that I would be well equipped to navigate my own illness, or that I might be treated with a little more respect. However, as I went from doctor to doctor looking for answers, I discovered that nothing could have been further from the truth! Once a trusted health care professional, I was now simply a 'chronically ill person' and with my invisible and difficult-to-diagnose disease, I wasn't always believed. Even worse, I could feel that I was looked down upon, and deemed to be a somewhat hysterical middle-aged, peri-menopausal woman. I had seen it happen with some of my patients, and now I understood the frustration and humiliation firsthand.

We are human. Our bodies get sick and they age, and yet society fears and rejects these processes and anything else that is beyond our control. For a very long time, I felt exiled from the world of the well. Being chronically sick made me feel isolated, an 'outsider'!

The health and disability insurers were more concerned about having a label than anything else. My own needs and my failing body seemed virtually irrelevant as they kept asking me to jump through hoops to 'prove' I was sick. I just wanted to walk away from it all, and yet I felt responsible. My husband and I had both lost our steady incomes due to my illness. The burden of guilt, frustration and shame was tremendous.

I did not understand why I couldn't get well. Wasn't illness a temporary thing? With the sudden onset I had experienced, would it not just peter out one day and I would be me again? Surely I wouldn't have to live like this forever? Do sick people sometimes just stay sick? These unanswered questions swam around in my brain like an unwelcome undercurrent of doom. I was in a deep dark hole with no ladder in sight.

The pace of my life had come to a dramatic halt. Since leaving work, it felt like my illness had become my job! I spent a lot of time and energy trying to work this all out. I tried to appreciate the small pleasures, like sunsets, flowers and birdsong. Nature was indeed my friend – mostly from my window, but I sat in my little garden whenever I was able. It was a great joy to feel the grass beneath my feet, or even sand between my toes. Where we live, it is possible to drive our vehicle right onto the local beach. This was such a blessing, especially on days when my physical exhaustion and brain fog did not allow me to 'do' anything.

From an early age, I had been very independent. I had always been the 'giver' in my life and not so good at receiving. Needing and accepting so much help and care was not at all easy for me. I chastised myself for being weak, even a failure! I felt vulnerable and exposed. But my reliance on others was also a lesson in how connected and interdependent we all are. We need our tribe, and social interaction is in fact vital for our wellbeing, yet in this situation I felt totally withdrawn. I didn't even know who I was anymore.

I found some personal notes that I made in my diary about how I was feeling at that time, so please allow me to share them with you:

'It seems that my appearance belies the pain that lies beneath! I am repeatedly told how well I look when I feel so poorly. I can see it when I look in the mirror. My eyes tell all. Why can others not see this, or are they just being polite? I want them all to understand that I am not being deliberately anti-social, and that even a lunch date with dear friends can take a huge toll on me. I put on the brave face but I pay a big price. It is always a trade-off!'

Journaling my feelings like this was helpful. In May 2008, I wrote this lengthier account of my predicament:

'I have had to abandon my career, but I will not give up on the JOY of life! This condition (ME) has taken so much away, for my husband as well. But I know it's important to hang on to what we have, especially when it's a loving, supportive relationship like ours.

It is such a burden living as the 'sick' family member. It makes me feel guilty and sad. I know it is difficult for others to understand how I can be so unwell without showing obvious outward physical signs. My body does not look broken to others. But in public I wear my 'happy face'. No one else sees the real me, struggling with this unwelcome demon that has invaded my body.

My husband is the one person who truly knows how sick I have become. His encouragement, patience and support are a great blessing and keep me going forward. My friends don't seem to understand my struggles, but I am just trying to survive.

My quest for a cure has led me to too many tests and drugs and lifestyle changes, and years of disappointments. I am distrusting of the medical profession now and I feel quite hopeless. Every minute of every day seems to revolve around my illness as I have given up so much. I have forgotten what it was like to wake up and simply live my life.

This interminable pain in my head blocks my thinking and saps my energy. It is completely intrusive in my daily life. I guess I have to realise that there may never be a cure for this problem, and that it might never go away. It makes me feel very isolated, as if no one knows what I am going through. My career, personal and financial life are all in tatters.

Much of my suffering now stems not just from the symptoms of the illness, but from the continuous roller coaster of frustration, havoc and despair that it has created in so many facets of my life.

Everything is now a challenge. From completing the most routine chore, to making plans with friends and keeping them! I am always in conflict about 'pushing through', or should I just give in? My old self is gone and I have not quite figured out how to piece together a new version to replace her.

I am aware that all pain can inhibit productivity. But head pain like this, felt in the brain, and so relentless, has the additional challenge of interfering with how I think. I have no energy to deal with the unpredictable. The headache is all I can handle.

I worry that it may be firmly imprinted in my central nervous system, never to be erased.

Besides the pain, there is always a sense of heaviness that I am pushing through, in order to do anything, and even to think! On rare 'better' days I naturally do more, but worse pain and fatigue will follow for the entire next day or even longer. Sometimes when I find myself behaving normally and having a good time out with friends, a cloud of dread will suddenly envelop me. There is always a delayed reaction. How big a price will I pay this time?

With my illness, there is such a blocking of energy. Perhaps I need to turn to Buddhism, where pain and suffering are an accepted part of life, and simply strive for inner peace.'

When I read this now, it is clear to me that I was stuck in a 'victim mentality', but I didn't know that at the time. It is apparent, looking back, that I wanted to be understood. I don't think I was looking for sympathy. Rather, I felt that other people acknowledging my misery would give it validation.

For a long while, I wanted to explain to everyone what had happened to me! But, of course, they didn't want to hear. Perhaps I was sensing what I found out much later to be true – that many didn't believe I was sick. Some friends had even brushed it off as an 'irrational breakdown'. It still hurts to realise that, but I can't blame them. It was a very confusing time.

I stumbled across a YouTube video that was the best thing I had found at clearly explaining this wretched disease and the toll it takes on people. I was still desperate for my loved ones to understand what was really going on, so when my parents next visited, I sat them down in front of my computer and played the clip. I was devastated when my dad got up and left the room halfway through. My heart sank. It felt like he didn't care enough.

Looking back, I see it very differently. I'm pretty sure that it was just too painful for him to hear the truth about how my body was letting me down, the lack of any effective treatment, the severity of my symptoms, and the poor prognosis. Of course he didn't want to hear this about his baby girl! He had always loved my zest for life, my sporting pursuits and my laugh.

After I got sick, my mum told me many times that she missed my laugh, but I just wasn't finding much to laugh about anymore. I didn't have the energy. The light had also gone from my eyes. Mum often said, 'Your eyes look tired, dear.' She and I seemed to be the only ones who recognised this.

If I only had a penny for every time someone told me, 'But you look so well!'

I started to write blogs, further documenting my feelings, and shared them online hoping that my words might help others. Our compassion for others deepens through our own experience of grief, doesn't it? Everything I wrote was also to help me, of course! Always listen to your own advice.

BLOG

'MY LIFE, YOUR LIFE. WE ARE ALL IN THE SAME BOAT!'

'Sometimes I feel very 'alone', as if I'm the only one going through whatever is happening in my life. I know that this is never true, but it is a disturbing feeling of isolation – that it's not worth discussing with anyone else, because it's just me!

This raises two issues:
First, that it is always a good idea to discuss your worries and emotions with others. 'A problem shared is a problem halved,' as they say. Did you know that all emotions we experience are universal, and any thought you ever have has been thought by others as well?

The sense of community when you know that someone cares – when they are prepared to listen, or even just offer a shoulder to cry on, is uplifting and invaluable to our self-worth. I will never forget the kindness of one caring friend who called me almost every week to offer support. Sheila was prepared to listen to all my latest trials and tribulations! I may not have always welcomed our chats, because speaking felt like hard work some days, but I am sure that I always felt better afterwards, knowing that I was loved.

We can feel quite vulnerable when we reach out and show our true selves to others, but it is always worthwhile, and we often find that they have felt this way too. They may not have solutions, but they understand what you are going through, and they do not judge you – even though you worried that they might see you as weak, or your issues as trivial.

Being able to voice your concerns, even write them down if you don't have someone to confide in, will remove that heavy energy that you have been carrying around inside you. Thinking out loud in this way can make you feel lighter and happier.

Second, the most important relationship we have is the one with ourselves. So, if we are feeling lost, overwhelmed or stuck, we need to get out of our heads; quiet the logical mind and the ego thoughts and connect with our true self – the essence that resides within the heart space, our soul chamber. Our divinity and infinite wisdom.

To facilitate this, I like to be in nature or play soothing music, close my eyes, breathe deeply and feel the connection. Just allowing myself to BE. Letting go for a short while, of any busy-ness. No doing or trying, just stillness.

Often, insights will come forth. Answers to unspoken questions, that help me to move forward. Sometimes I sense colours that I allow myself to absorb and enjoy. At times like this, I can feel like I am ONE with my soul – the eternal inner me who does not judge, loves unconditionally and holds all the answers.'

***

Before this, I had been looking outside of myself for answers. It had been a lifelong habit, and one that I ultimately needed to change. I felt the pressure of obligation, and a need to defend myself and explain my choices. This was like apologising for who I was, and it was further draining my inner power. I needed to drop the judgment about what could or should have happened in the past, and not drag it with me into the future.

I needed to change my reality from the inside out. I had to learn to value myself for simply being me, and not by how much I could 'achieve' each day – as I had been unwittingly prone to do.

PART TWO

HEALING FROM WITHIN – AN INTEGRATIVE APPROACH

CHAPTER 6

The MIND
(Our Thoughts Create Our Reality)

'SET PEACE OF MIND AS YOUR HIGHEST GOAL AND ORGANISE YOUR LIFE AROUND IT.' **- BRIAN TRACY**

In 2009, I discovered Ashok Gupta, a UK doctor who had been touched by CFS himself and developed an Amygdala (reptilian brain) Retraining Program that was full of good advice. It explained how the central nervous system was always on high alert and over-stimulated. I started to understand how the negative thoughts about my situation caused adrenaline and other stress chemicals to be released, which would then exacerbate my symptoms, and lead right back to more negative thoughts. A very counter-productive 'vicious cycle' indeed.

MY NEGATIVE THOUGHTS AND HOW I TURNED THEM AROUND

I kept a 'negative thoughts' diary. Here are some of the major ones I came to recognise:

* I have had this illness for so long. How can I ever get better?

* I have read that only five per cent of people recover.

* Only the young ones get over this illness.

* I have had a constant headache for over six years. How could this ever go away?

* Nobody understands how sick I am.

* My brain scans have shown extensive damage. How can I recover from this?

* My eyes hurt all the time. I just want to close them!

* I want to go for a walk but I'm worried about how I will feel after.

I was being bombarded with these fear-based thoughts all the time and had to find a way to interrupt rather than indulge them. I learned to say 'STOP, STOP, STOP' in my head, take a deep breath, smile, and imagine feeling good. This was a helpful reset that I did many, many times per day at first, but needed less as time went by.

I learned how to turn my negative thinking into being more aligned with love – compassionate, optimistic and uplifting. Thoughts that put a smile on your face don't drain your energy and are more conducive for health and happiness.

A young psychic friend urged me to set up a Facebook page to share health tips and messages of inspiration. Little did I know that it would connect me with thousands of like-hearted souls from all around the world.

Positive affirmations are supportive words you can repeat to yourself in order to create positive change. A kind of 'fake it 'til you make it' idea – stating them until you believe. They can assist by overriding our subconscious self-sabotaging negativity.

This is an example of a post I shared offering a helpful positive affirmation:

> 'Today I tune in to the flow of life. I surrender and allow myself to step into what is needed. I release any urge to push or force, I let go of 'shoulds' and 'musts' and move forward with hope in my heart. I am patient with myself and trust that healing will occur on all levels.'

MANTRAS FOR HEALTH – POSITIVE AFFIRMATIONS THAT HAVE HELPED ME:

* My body now restores itself to its natural state of perfect health.

* Life is wonderful; I feel great.

* I am love, I am light and I am safe.

* Everything is happening for me, not to me.

* I trust myself as I make choices that are taking me in the right direction.

* I love and fully accept myself. I see myself through eyes of love.

* I am grateful for this body that carries me through life.

* Good things come from change. I embrace the unknown.

* I am strong and resourceful. I can overcome all challenges that come my way.

Eventually my body started to change. I didn't always need the twelve to fourteen hours of sleep every day. Sometimes, I could stroll on the beach for a few minutes without being bed-ridden for the next two days. Things were looking up.

In 2008, I read about a woman who had a chronic daily headache for seventeen years! I was five years into mine at this point. But the Eastern medicine approach struck a chord with me. They described head pain as a symptom of a much larger problem, a 'greater weakening of the body', such as life force energy (Chi) getting stuck at a pre-existing weak point in the body, with pain and dysfunction.

I wondered if there was a link back to the head injury I had experienced at seventeen, when I was thrown out of a car in an accident. My quest for answers continued. I tried acupuncture, which is said to unblock the Chi, and various other modalities such as cranio-sacral therapy, bio-resonance and theta healing – all of which were previously unknown to me. I could see value in their holistic, mind-body-spirit approach.

In time, my quest for health became a gradual rediscovery of my natural state of wellbeing. I had to learn to relax and enjoy the unfolding. It was still a roller coaster, but I was starting to believe that I would get well. That was a huge step in the right direction. I had been looking for a CURE (something that I thought someone else would provide for me) but it became clear that I had to look inside of me for true HEALING to begin.

The journal note I had penned about striving for inner peace proved to be quite prophetic! In learning how to reach inner peace, so many other aspects of my life benefited too. Every aspect, in fact.

DISCOVERING MEDITATION

Meditation was a lifeline. I felt lost and agitated, even angry at times; frustrated by a body that continually let me down despite my best efforts, but I tried to keep smiling. Sitting quietly and allowing my mind to settle calmed my nervous system and eased the headache.

I joined a meditation group where I made some new friends and found more coping skills. I now had something to look forward to each week. The group leader, Rosalie, highlighted a few things I could work on: self-love in particular. I meditated every day and got strong messages of reassurance that I was on the right path.

I became aware that the angels are our celestial friends and were always with me, and I learned to trust in a connection with higher realms. I could feel my nana's presence around me for the first time since she passed many years before. Just after my first grandson was born, she came to me in a meditation, shrouded me in love and passed the baton! She told me it was my turn to be Nana now. This was a very special experience that I was certainly not expecting, and moments like these bolstered my heart and fuelled my interest in exploring further.

How poignant I realised, that my disease ME would lead me back to the real me! You've got to love the irony of the Universe. My sense of humour was coming back. And here I was with an invisible disease, discovering another invisible reality. The heart and mind are capable of expanding in ways I had never thought possible.

BLOG

'YOUR HEALTH AND HAPPINESS ARE IN YOUR HANDS'

'Did you know that your thoughts are the key to your health? Learn to monitor them and recognise when they are being counterproductive. Then you can switch them around and choose thoughts that make you FEEL better in that moment. It's a bit of a process, but a logical one and well worth the effort. Embrace the learning curve.

Your heart needs to feel nurtured, and your soul wants to be calm. Do not create turmoil by dwelling on upsetting memories. As you replay them in your head, your body responds and will suffer. Find your way to 'better feeling' thoughts as often as you can. Choose words that shift you to a happier place, where your stress hormones will not set off a cascade of physiological responses that are averse to your wellbeing.

Your health and happiness are in your hands. It's empowering to know this. When you don't like how you are feeling – anxious, worried or down – scan your thoughts. Where has your primary focus been? There is probably a direct link, and you can potentially flip the situation by simply recognising this and choosing a different focus. Don't expect to go from miserable to elated in five deep breaths, but you will certainly step it up a notch by moving towards what you desire.

Be still and put on a fake smile. Fill your heart with love and compassion for just a moment. Visualise a time when you felt these deeply – maybe it was when you held a newborn baby or a tiny helpless kitten. Find a memory like this that will trigger a higher vibration within you. Be gentle with yourself, not frustrated or judgmental. Accept your humanness and laugh at your 'mistakes'. You can use this shift to move your health forward as well – find a memory or invent a scene that you can go to in your mind's eye and make an effort to see and feel this whenever you need it. Turn up the colour and sound and use all of your senses, in your imagination.

When I was trapped in my Chronic Fatigue phase, I learned to do this, and found it very beneficial. When I was having a 'poor me' moment, dwelling on how exhausted, weak and sad I felt, I would STOP, close my eyes, and go back to my water-skiing days. I could really feel how strong I was as I skimmed across the water on my single ski, leaning back and cutting through the wake with a big smile. I could feel the sunshine and the spray of the water on my face as I visualised it all. I felt happy and strong and very alive! And I was proud of my achievements. As I relived it all, I may have become much more skilled than I actually was too. The magical power of the mind.

I only needed to do this for a few moments at a time. It was my magic reset point – and it cut short my suffering, which was clearly happening in my mind. Find your own pivot point and don't overthink it. A helpful image may pop easily into your head and it will feel right. Store it away. Then, when you recognise a moment that you need it, Stop, *close* your eyes, *visualise, feel, breathe* it in deeply and don't forget to *smile*.'

***

Perhaps intuition is the highest form of intelligence: hunches, gut instinct, intellectual curiosity (with a hunger for the pursuit of knowledge), and a willingness for growth and exploration of previous assumptions. Instead of the mind telling the heart how to feel, it may be more beneficial to invite the heart to instruct the mind how to respond to the life around us. The programmed mind can be a tyrant; it will play tricks on us and tell us lies. The heart and light within us never do. We must remember that we are born with all that we need.

Albert Einstein will always be an inspirational icon. A favourite quote of his is 'Imagination is everything. It is the preview of life's coming attractions.' The mind is powerful and can generate images that translate into our reality. Hence, it is prudent to learn to create the stories that we want for ourselves. Our most dominant thoughts always come to the forefront. Become aware of whether your focus is bringing you closer to your desired state of being, or further away.

Healing and transformation are only possible when we change our perspectives from within and allow our pain to meaningfully rewrite our life story. As we release our judgment about what could or should have happened in the past, we change our reality from the inside out, dropping the weights that were stopping us from moving ahead. After all, we can't solve a problem by using the same mindset that created it!

The mind tends to have a narrow focus, but wisdom brings greater awareness of the bigger picture and how everything is connected. The human voice has many opinions, but our power lies in the soul voice. For wisdom, we must tap into that, aligning head with heart. When thoughts subside, creativity and insight can emanate from our consciousness, helping us to solve our problems and leading us toward a more joyful existence. We start to live with greater compassion and unconditional love, which are inherent aspects of our essence. We can see beyond our personality and our conditioning and are able to recognise the light within ourselves and all others, no matter what. (Even in 'difficult' people who seem to keep their light well hidden.)

It's all about learning to quiet the noise and amplify the inner guidance, bringing a helpful synergy between the inner world and external world, which we are, in fact, creating. We learn to respond with loving kindness rather than react from fear or pain. As we each do this, perhaps as a species we will move away from conflict and division and into greater cooperation and unity.

TOXIC EMOTIONS

Emotions can be toxic, too. Fear, for example, is a very limiting emotion. It is disempowering and holds us back from a myriad of possibilities. We all have fears that are long-held and not always logical. And we each experience fear on many different levels: fear of the unknown, fear of not being good enough, fear of speaking up, fear of being disliked, and so on (these ones have certainly been some of mine).

Let's not be afraid of our fears! They are valid because they exist, but perhaps if we start to recognise them, acknowledge them and even thank them, they may dissipate and transform. Their power over us may abate or even vanish. We will see from a new perspective. Nothing changes, yet everything is different. It is all about perception. American president Franklin D. Roosevelt said, in his first inaugural address, 'There is nothing to fear but fear itself.' These are wise words that have always stuck with me.

There is a lot of dark energy in our world today, and it's hard to not buy into it. The media and world events are full of it. But, if we stay in tune with our own integrity, with our intentions pure and benevolent, then our thoughts, actions and deeds will remain loving and kind. When we tap into the flow of life force energy that is coursing through us, we radiate our light and keep our vibration high. This is also an energy of love, which can always dispel fear. I like to think of love and fear as two sides of a coin, which cannot present together.

Love is the light that expels the darkness of fear. This is the attitude that I feel our planet needs more of. It transcends all boundaries and can permeate all cultures and religions. Even politics and big business! Imagine if this premise was intrinsic. How different the world would be. I like to hold the vision, and believe that this is the way forward.

CHAPTER 7

The BODY
(Food, Nutrition and the Gut-Brain Connection)

'YOU CAN'T KEEP ONE DISEASE AND HEAL TWO OTHERS. WHEN THE BODY HEALS, IT HEALS EVERYTHING' **– CHARLOTTE GERSON**

Hippocrates, the ancient Greek physician (also known as the 'Father of Medicine') said, 'Let food be thy medicine and medicine be thy food.' This quote is thousands of years old but highlights the importance of healthy eating and how the nutrients in various foods have healing properties.

I have discovered that true healing is about letting go of the need to find a cure, and instead allowing the body to repair from the inside out. Hence, the new name of my private practice, 'Healing from Within' and my catchphrase 'Simple Strategies for Health and Happiness'.

But what does true health and happiness really mean, you may ask? Well, positive health is certainly not just the absence of disease. It is an innate vitality, energy and zest for life. Our human body wants to be WELL! It is always striving for homeostasis, to return to its natural state of good health. But in today's world, we place a lot of obstacles in our way; some we may be aware of, others not. What if we were to remove those obstacles and trust in the amazing ability of the body to repair, restore and regenerate? Could it be as simple as this? Perhaps it is. We are very prone to overcomplicate things, after all.

In the 21st century, we are chronically sicker than ever before! Despite all of the education, research and modern treatment facilities, we don't seem to be winning. Modern metabolic diseases are on the rise, and they all have common links to nutrition and lifestyle choices. What on earth are we doing to ourselves? We are in an epidemic of chronic disease. And have you noticed that wild animals do not die from human diseases, but our domesticated animals now do? This is a scary observation.

Have you heard of the world's Blue Zones? The people in these five unique communities live longer, happier and healthier lives than others on our planet. And guess what, the common thread between them all is their diet and lifestyle choices, and their community spirit. There is much we can learn from them. The power of food and love, we might say. In essence, we can all create our own personal Blue Zone once we are aware of the factors.

FUNDAMENTAL PRINCIPLES OF HEALTH

Exercise is vital for good health. The lymph system has no pump of its own, yet it is a vital part of our excretory system. We need to move the body regularly to release hormones and remove waste. Movement helps us to avoid or recover from constipation, too. Keep it simple and do what you enjoy so that exercise is not a chore.

Did you know that our 'happy hormones' rely on a healthy gut? So does a strong immune system, and where do harmful chemicals fit into the equation? You are probably aware of the benefits of eating organic – as all foods used to be! – or removing processed foods from your plate, especially the ones with added 'numbers'. These man-made additives, which the human body cannot utilise, are not 'food'. The body will cleverly recognise them as foreign and potentially harmful, and use up a lot of energy and resources trying to clear them from our system.

It is helpful to have a reference guide close at hand when shopping. It can be tricky, even deceptive, as some foods are exempt from labelling. I once purchased a salad sandwich on a domestic flight and was shocked to find twenty seven listed ingredients, and many were flavour enhancers and preservatives! Why? There appears to be little regard for nutrition – only for taste, shelf life and profit. If lots of chemicals are going in, our poor body is always trying to detox (putting out fires, as I tend to think of it), and is therefore much less able to accomplish its 'healing' mission.

How disappointing that even in organic foods, the nutrient value is often sadly inadequate today. There are many influential factors that have caused this, including mineral-depleted modern soils, intensive farming and pesticide spraying, and current-day food practices like picking before ripe, prolonged storage and so forth. So, we really have our work cut out for us! The work of Dr Zach Bush and others on regenerative agriculture is a very enlightening. There is also a film series called *Farmer's Footprint* if you are interested to learn more.

In addition, even with the best diet, we will only be able to absorb the nutrition if the gut (gastro-intestinal tract) is healthy and digestion is optimal. How many of us can say that our gut is always happy, with no bloating, tummy pain, indigestion or reflux?

It all leads us to realise that we humans of today are facing a far greater toxic load than even fifty years ago, and much-reduced nutrition. This is not a good recipe for health. How sad that the current generation are likely to be the first to not outlive their parents. It is mind-blowing and simply not good enough.

THE GUT-BRAIN CONNECTION

My journey back to health has led me to learn a great deal about the digestive tract. We all understand that there is an undeniable relationship between what we eat and the way our body performs, right?

The gut-brain connection is now backed up by endless studies, but the best understanding is of course gained through your own experience. It is now evident that the connection is a two-way street, in that they influence one another. The nerve cells in the gut communicate with the brain at a much higher rate than vice versa. When they sense that all is well, the brain is signalled that there is no need for concern. But if there is anything amiss – like infection, inflammation or altered microbial population (dysbiosis) – the nerves signal the brain that there is trouble. This can result in pain, stress and other chronic gastrointestinal issues like Irritable Bowel Syndrome (IBS) or gastric reflux.

There is an inner ecosystem in the gastro-intestinal tract called the MICROBIOME. It consists of a complex web of bacteria, yeast, enzymes, neurochemicals, gut linings and cells belonging to the immune system. It is crucial to maintain health and balance here. The integrity of the gut is vital in order to absorb and utilise necessary nutrients. Even with a good diet, we can have malnutrition if our digestive health is poor. Consequently, many of us today are overfed and undernourished!

THE CONNECTION BETWEEN GUT HEALTH AND MENTAL ILLNESS

You are probably aware that mental illness is prolific. While it remains a medical field full of mysteries, and many of these illnesses are diagnostically difficult to establish, the link between the gut and brain is undeniable and becoming more widely understood. Studies into even the most severe forms of mental illness, and the benefits of diet and lifestyle changes, are yielding very positive results. I am pleased to say the research into probiotics and mental health is quite fascinating, leading the mainstream towards some of the more 'natural' methods that stem from ancient wisdom.

Is there really a 'chemical imbalance' in the brain? You are probably starting to understand that my approach is all about addressing the underlying cause. What if pharmaceuticals are just covering up symptoms, and what about their potential side effects? Sadly, we have all heard the adage 'the cure is worse than the complaint'. Surely it is always prudent to first explore treatment methods that do no harm.

Please be aware that it is never my intention to diagnose or prescribe. I am simply sharing with love my own research, experience and intuition – which have led me back to a better place. If you are feeling depressed, anxious or overwhelmed, always seek help from a health professional. You do not need to face this alone.

No matter what symptoms are presenting, let's get back to basics and give the body what it needs to heal the underlying cause. Of all the body systems, DIGESTION seems to have the biggest influence on mental health. The body uses up nutrients at a greater rate when we are under emotional STRESS, so topping up with nutritional support (such as colloidal minerals) and learning how to best manage our stress is very helpful. If you have never before made a link between nutrition and mental health, this could be a focus to consider. Happy hormones and mood regulators (like serotonin and dopamine) are made in a healthy gut wall. If your digestive tract is populated with the wrong bacteria, you probably won't be able to make enough of the 'feel good' chemicals you need.

LEAKY GUT

Have you heard of Leaky Gut Syndrome (LGS)? It's a funny name for an all-too-common condition. LGS occurs when there is a damaged gut lining, creating increased permeability of the intestinal wall. This allows macro-molecules and foreign bodies to enter the bloodstream, causing oxidative stress and an autoimmune response that drives chronic inflammation throughout the body. This often leads to joint pains, thyroid problems and a myriad of other complaints. Leaky gut is often implicated in an array of autoimmune and mental health issues. It starts in the small intestine but, in time, affects the whole body.

How do you know if you have LGS? The first clue is often food intolerances. Another is a deficiency of vitamins or minerals such as magnesium, iron or B12 – which appears to be so common now! Skin conditions like eczema and dermatitis should raise red flags, too. Later consequences can be thyroid dysfunction, Rheumatoid Arthritis and other autoimmune diseases like Fibromyalgia and Chronic Fatigue Syndrome.

FOODS THAT HELP OR HINDER

So, what do we do? It is imperative that we eat **REAL FOOD**, as opposed to the vast array of highly processed commercial materials in our supermarkets that are more like 'fake food'. There are also many genetically modified 'foods' that some would call Frankenfoods! Choose whole foods with as little human intervention as possible.

Drink **CLEAN WATER**, hydrating with at least 30mls/kg body weight per day. Ideally spring water, and certainly fluoride and chlorine free (as these can contribute to thyroid issues).

Use whole **SALT**. Pink Himalayan rock salt is my favourite, delicious and nutritious, and Celtic Sea salt comes from relatively unpolluted waters.

Remove processed **SUGAR** (and flour) from your diet, as it creates an insulin roller coaster. Keep your blood sugars more stable with clean eating and whole foods (single ingredient), and you will also notice more emotional stability and less pronounced mood swings. Sugar suppresses the immune system and feeds yeast, and yeast overgrowth (candida) attacks the gut wall.

Modern **WHEAT** is very high in gluten, which is known to damage the integrity of the bowel. There is no clear nutritional value in gluten, and you may feel a great deal better without it. Bread today is very high in gluten, which not only contributes to leaky gut but is known to destroy the myelin sheath (the protective coating on nerves). You might recall that this type of damage showed up on my MRI as extensive scarring in my brain!

When I stopped eating bread, my heart palpitations ceased. My ongoing sinus issues improved greatly too! Today's gluten is often genetically modified and highly addictive, therefore contributing to obesity. Why not explore options within nutritious gluten free grains such as brown rice, amaranth and millet, and also seeds like quinoa and buckwheat (which despite its name is gluten free and unrelated to wheat). You may discover some that you enjoy.

EAT to keep the body alkaline, your hormones balanced, and reduce systemic inflammation – which underpins all chronic disease. Inflammatory foods to be aware of and try to limit: sugars, artificial sweeteners, cooking oils, trans fats, dairy products, processed meats, alcohol, all wheat and gluten grains, and artificial food additives.

If you are assuming that **DAIRY** products help your bones, please consider that the UK, USA and Australia consume more dairy than anywhere else in the world, and yet these countries have the highest rates of osteoporosis (poor bone density and strength). Unfortunately, dairy products today are often highly processed and difficult to digest and are likely to contain antibiotics (which we know are damaging to the digestive tract). Many people are also lactose (milk sugar) and casein (milk protein) intolerant.

Food is information for the body, as well as fuel, so we need to treat it with respect. Choose **ORGANIC** where possible, as chemical sprays will destroy beneficial microbes.

Some beneficial foods to consider including in your diet are:

* Bone broth, a perfect food full of amino acids.

* Unrefined coconut oil, which has antimicrobial and antioxidant properties.

* Sauerkraut (sulphur rich) and other fermented foods and kefirs.

* Blueberries, green tea and other foods high in antioxidants.

* All brightly-coloured vegetables, particularly leafy greens.

NUTRITIONAL SUPPLEMENTS

We must give the body the essentials it needs to function well, so we should consider nutritional support in the form of supplements. This may not have been necessary twenty to thirty years ago, but I have had to concede that it now is, especially for things like minerals, which our bodies can't make. With adequate minerals on board, the body is better able to break down toxins, do its job of repairing, and manufacture almost everything else we need such as vitamins, hormones, and enzymes.

As always, be discerning when you search for the best nutritional supplements and other safe products. Seek out ethical companies that produce high quality, effective and planet-friendly items.

A cheeky clue: it's probably not the companies that spend the most on advertising. Always aim to choose a quality nutritional supplement of practitioner strength.

Some highly effective nutritional supplements have made a huge difference for me and my family. There is no 'one size fits all' recipe, but here are some of my personal favourites to consider:

PROBIOTICS: Bacterial dysbiosis is an imbalance in the ratio of beneficial bacteria to others within the microbiome. This is always problematic and there is now overwhelming evidence that we need to promote the growth of helpful (over harmful) gut bugs. Pre- and pro-biotics will offer protection for the gut lining, improve digestion, and boost the production of important B vitamins.

MINERALS: Micro-minerals can bypass the digestive system and act like a tonic for the blood. Micronutrients can also stave off cravings and boost our ability to make wiser food choices.

DIGESTIVE ENZYMES: These can be a helpful supplement at specific times, such as right after a heavy meal, or a meal you know is not ideal (like meat and starches together). They will give your gut a rest by helping to break down the food, gluten and other compounds.

COLOSTRUM: When leaky gut is present, I have found that a quality colostrum supplement can work in synergy with probiotics to effectively lower inflammation and restore the integrity of the gut wall. This works toward a long-term solution by addressing the underlying cause and not just reducing symptoms. Did you know that all babies are born with leaky gut, and it is the colostrum from breast milk that shuts it down? Nature is always perfection and can teach us a lot.

TOXIC CHEMICALS IN PERSONAL CARE AND IN THE HOME

In 2013, I met a lovely lady called Glenys who taught me that ingesting chemicals through food is only part of the story. She was devoted to education about natural health, giving wellness presentations and supporting people through illness. I learned a great deal from Glenys and am forever grateful.

Are you aware that there are thousands of man-made chemicals we inhale, or absorb through our skin? Many are in our environment (air, water, even clothing and home furnishings), but there are many we bring into the home ourselves and can avoid once we become aware and empowered to make better choices.

We all regularly purchase products – cleaning, bathroom, skincare and cosmetics – that may be making us sick, or at least hindering us from being completely well. Hundreds, even thousands of potentially harmful ingredients are commonly in these commercial products, and our bodies are working overtime to deal with them, trying to keep us well and often losing the battle.

After years of research, I am now able to make informed choices. I try to purchase from ethical brands and fill our home with only safe, non-toxic bathroom, household and personal care products. It takes less than thirty seconds for chemicals to get into the bloodstream and have an adverse effect on the gut and other major organs. Please be especially vigilant about toothpaste, mouthwash, hair products and face creams, which are absorbed near the brain.

Insect repellent and fly sprays are likely to contain DEET, which is a neurotoxin, so it is best avoided on the body or in the home. I know of one baby who developed seizures when her mum was using these products in a dispenser above the cot. She thought she was doing the right thing by protecting her baby from mosquitoes, but the consequence was dire. Baby's recovery was complete after the removal of the sprays, I am happy to report. So, please be aware of the possible impact of exposure to harmful chemicals, including pollutants, toxic additives, artificial colours, flavourings and fragrances. We are sensitive organisms to be treated with respect.

We are now seeing high levels of toxicity (and malnutrition) on live blood analysis, even in children, and large numbers of toxins are showing up in the cord blood of newborn babies. Luckily, most of these toxins are completely avoidable once we realise they are in products we are buying. Of course, when we know better, we do better.

When I discovered that my long-term favourite perfume (the one my husband so kindly gave me for each birthday) was actually full of nasty chemicals, I quickly turned to a natural essential oil blend as a beautiful, safe alternative. I was also horrified to discover that the high-profile skin care brand I used to purchase, was (and still is) tested on animals. How unnecessarily cruel!

I became aware too that the very common body lotion recommended to us as massage cream is a petrochemical by-product yet is widely promoted as 'low allergy'. Be careful what you believe. Please do your own research and choose with discernment from ethical brands – responsible companies that are considering you, and the environment, and producing safe products simply because they know it's the right thing to do. Too many companies are all about profit. More will no doubt produce ethical products when they realise that's what we consumers want to purchase. We must vote where our power lies: with our shopping dollars.

We can never be sure what percentage of getting well is about removing toxins from our homes. I do know that it was an important piece of the puzzle in my own case, and for many others I have since met. Once the physical 'irritants' are gone, we feel stronger and more positive and upbeat.

Whatever your predicament, there is no magic bullet, but wise diet and lifestyle choices make a huge difference. There is no doubt that nutritional support, along with avoidance of harmful chemicals, is always a valuable adjunct to other self-help strategies. I have seen many astounding turnarounds in health and wellbeing with this approach – often with unexpected transformation in self-esteem and zest for life as a side benefit.

Consider the benefits of addressing these issues in your own life. The missing pieces of your unique health puzzle may then be able to fall into place.

BLOG

'GETTING BACK TO GOOD HABITS'

'Today I am starting a reset! For the past few weeks I have been feeling frustrated with myself, as my usual commitment to looking after myself and leading by example have taken a big hit.

It was all very logical, really – for many months my own life was largely taken over by caring for my elderly parents. And I didn't mind that, but my own needs rapidly slid well down the list of priorities and that eventually took its toll.

There were many aspects to this. Food was a big one. I was having to stay away from home a lot, so I no longer had such tight control of what went onto my plate. There were lots of cafe stops while visiting Dad in hospital and eating on the run. I thought I was making the best choices I could, but the menus weren't always geared to healthy options.

The mental strain was also exhausting. So, even when I had the time and means to choose well, I didn't always have the energy or resolve.

While Dad was in hospital, and fighting so hard to stay with us, nothing actually felt too difficult. I surprised myself with how well I coped with the gruelling schedule and emotional roller coaster. I was grateful for the skills I had acquired that served me so well, and I just kept putting one foot in front of the other.

But when Dad passed away, it was a big game changer, and suddenly everything felt too hard. I held it together long enough for us to honour him with a fitting farewell, but after the funeral I felt completely adrift. I was unable to tackle my everyday tasks – in fact, I didn't even want to!

I knew what I needed in order to get back on track – meditation, walks on the beach and clean eating. But I am also aware that grieving doesn't wait for anyone, so I have tried to just allow it to unfold. It's only been six weeks (as I write this) after all.

However, I have been beating myself up about what wasn't getting done. And of course, that was making me feel worse! So, I have let all of that go now, and started to be more kind to myself. And with the support of wonderful family and friends, I am gradually regaining the strength to embrace again the life that I want for myself.

Having recently witnessed a lot of hospital procedures and medical interventions, has made me even more determined to spread the word about taking responsibility for our own health: awareness and prevention, natural methods, ancient wisdom and getting back to basics. And today feels like a new start for me too!

Today I have been out for an early walk and am starting the day with a delicious green juice. I need to restock the fridge but this one is just what we had at hand – spinach, parsley and mint from our garden, with an apple, cucumber and small piece of fresh ginger. Yum. My body was craving a nutritious juice and it has really hit the spot.

I have also been aware how caffeinated tea has crept right back into my repertoire. Often this was all that was available during our long stints at the hospital, but now I intend to get back to mostly herbal teas, which luckily, I do enjoy. Perhaps you have some favourites too, and carry them with you?

Fortunately, I have kept up my nutritional supplement regime and I've been able to remain physically well, but I have certainly lost my equilibrium. So now I will endeavour to put all the pieces back together. I will carry raw nuts and vegetable sticks with me everywhere, so that I am not tempted by gluten or sugar filled snacks. And I will continue to drink adequate clean (spring) water every day, between meals. I will nourish my body and soul with what I know I need, and not what my head may be telling me is an 'easier' option. It is of course not worth it if it makes you feel poorly.'

***

HEALTHY FOOD HABITS

I am aware that in today's world, life is very full, and we may often feel too busy to make the best choices. But I want you to know that healthy eating is not just about willpower and determination!

I am going to share some tricks of the trade that I learned along the way. As I researched more about the link between food, nutrition and vitality, I created a list of helpful tips. Perhaps you will find that you can create some healthful new habits, rather than just trying to exercise restraint.

1) CROWD OUT THE BAD STUFF

Make a list of all the healthy foods you like and stock your fridge and pantry with those. You won't eat the rubbish if it's not in front of you. Choose whole foods (one ingredient, unadulterated) like fruit and vegetables, raw nuts and seeds, and quality animal protein (eggs, meat and seafood). Fill yourself up on foods that are tasty and nutritious, then you won't be hungry or feel deprived. Carry snacks everywhere so you're not tempted to buy 'convenience' foods when out and about – vegetable sticks, a piece of fruit, or nuts and seeds can save the day! I always do this on flights now too, as airline meals tend to be heavy and highly processed.

2) DRINK ADEQUATE WATER

Hydrate, hydrate, hydrate! Our bodies require a lot of water, and sometimes when you feel hungry, headachy or unwell, it may be partly because of dehydration. Try drinking a glass of lovely pure water, and wait twenty minutes to see if you feel better and any hunger subsides. Add a pinch of Himalayan salt to the water for improved absorption by the body. Drink between meals, not at the table. Drinking with food can undermine the potency of the digestive enzymes we need.

3) SHOP THE PERIMETER OF THE SUPERMARKET

Avoid the packaged 'food-like substances' that are highly processed and have a long list of ingredients and long shelf life. These are usually found in the more central aisles. Better still, seek farmers markets so that you are buying fresh, local and seasonal produce, and hopefully organic too. Involve your children/grandchildren in this, so that they learn the origin of what they eat and develop a fun relationship with food. If possible, plant a few things yourself. Herbs and leafy greens are so easy to grow organically, even in pots, and they are highly beneficial to consume.

4) MAXIMISE YOUR NUTRITION

Feeling hungry is the body craving nutrition – vitamins, minerals and trace elements. Our mind unfortunately goes to coffee, chocolate or ice cream! The body can manufacture most of what it needs when it is getting adequate mineral intake, but as this is unlikely to come from today's food, you might consider a quality nutritional supplement. You won't be so hungry (or moody!) when you have enough minerals on board.

5) LOVE YOURSELF MORE

Eating well is an act of self-love. This may require you to examine your thoughts about whether you deserve to be happy and healthy. Sometimes long-held beliefs are not serving us well. Work on loving and fully accepting yourself. You are always doing the best you can with what you know. When you care more about yourself, you automatically nurture your real needs, and move towards what you truly require. This is a powerful tool to have. When I first started to eat cleanly, when eating out I would look at the menu and get really disappointed if there was only one thing I could eat and it wasn't what I felt like! Now when I eat out, if there is one thing on the menu that is a good choice for me, I am ecstatic and grateful. It's all about perspective; re-framing things in the mind can make every experience more enjoyable.

6) MAKE COOKING FUN

Preparing healthy, life-enhancing food does not have to be a difficult or dreaded chore. It is a great act of love and can bring much enjoyment. Recruit some help from loved ones and engage them in simple tasks like washing or chopping vegetables. You will find yourselves communicating in ways that don't happen at other times. Play your favourite music and put a smile on your face. Enjoy the process; be fully present and connected to your food. And get creative! Start with a recipe if you wish but learn to trust your intuition and add flavours you know you like. Enjoy the feast for your senses, especially the colours and delicious aromas as you cook, which is all part of the pre-digestion process.

I do hope you will try to implement some of these tips. Please pick and choose from whatever inspires you. I would love to hear how you go.

CHAPTER 8

The SPIRIT
(Intuition and Psychic Senses)

'THE INTUITIVE MIND IS A SACRED GIFT, AND THE RATIONAL MIND IS A FAITHFUL SERVANT. WE HAVE CREATED A SOCIETY THAT HONOURS THE SERVANT AND HAS FORGOTTEN THE GIFT.'
– ALBERT EINSTEIN

A *Course in Miracles* teaches us: 'Enlightenment is not change. It is simply a recognition of what is already there.' There are always layers and textures within our life choices, but your roadmap will emerge as you begin to trust yourself again. People, ideas and contacts will start to flow into your awareness – and your heart will be awakened to the blessings within it all. There is always a silver lining. At some point you will find yourself hurtling towards what you want, rather than running away from what you don't!

Our instincts become sharpest when we need them the most – when we are navigating turbulence. The more we follow our intuition, the more doors will open to help us fulfil our life purpose.

Things started to turn around for me after a second, more

damning diagnosis. This time it was not only life changing, but also life threatening! I had a malignant melanoma (skin cancer), which had been present for quite a long time. I had pointed out this spot on my leg to my GP a couple of times, but she was not concerned about it. And when she did eventually send me to a skin specialist, they misdiagnosed it! My confidence in doctors was certainly being challenged.

Thank goodness I trusted my instincts and persisted until I finally found an experienced doctor who would listen. She determined right away what it was and performed an immediate excision and biopsy. I was also lucky that it had been very slow-growing. Prior to this, I had not known much about the characteristics of melanoma, but I'm so glad I followed my intuition – it really saved my life. If you have a mole that is changing shape or colour, has irregular margins, or is itchy or bleeding, these are all red flags. Please get it checked out by an expert.

I do sometimes wonder why I persevered for so long with a GP who did not appear to be helping me. But there was something deep inside of me that had always bowed to doctors, an ancestral reverence perhaps. On the other hand, back then I did not know that there were other beneficial approaches. My focus and belief system around health had been very narrow until this point, and I was also in a greatly weakened state, both physically and emotionally. I literally did not have the strength to make wise decisions for myself, so I deferred to those who I believed would 'know best'. But, of course, when it comes to what is best for you, no one knows better than you do!

I hit rock bottom in March 2009. I not only expected that the melanoma would kill me, but I also remember my initial reaction: *it would be a relief to die.* Here was my legitimate way out of the seemingly endless suffering. It hit me like a ton of bricks. I was really shocked and horrified that I could even think this way, so in that moment, I surrendered. I determined that even if I couldn't find a way to be well, I would not give up until I found a way to be happy.

And then, of course, the right people and resources started to come into my life and show me a new way forward. I recognised what was needed in order to change and take full responsibility for myself. Strategies and healing modalities also appeared to me, and I embraced everything that felt right and kept me moving in a positive direction. It seems I set a powerful intention that day. It was a defining moment for sure, and my ground zero became a launching pad for my success, as is so often the case.

I really believe that people and opportunities appear to us when we most need them. 'When the student is ready, the teacher will appear,' as they say. Soon after my subsequent surgery (a broad excision of the melanoma from my thigh), I met a new friend – let's call her Jasmine.

It was only a few days post-surgery, but something made me go to a meeting on the other side of town. I was still searching for answers for my Chronic Fatigue, so I found myself at yet another meeting of the local CFS/ME Society. My brilliant husband drove me once again, as I was not yet up to that task. To be honest, I was ready to give up on these gatherings, as they were largely attended by people who appeared to be well and truly stuck in their own misery, which I found to be quite depressing.

On this day, the speaker was again less than inspiring. However, another lady and her husband were sitting behind us, and at the tea break she asked me about the doctor I was seeing. We chatted about our health journeys and seemed to have a lot in common. The four of us talked in the car park for about an hour afterwards, and we exchanged numbers to keep in touch. Jasmine and I became firm friends, and she helped me a great deal. She will tell you that we actually helped each other, but Jasmine was far more open to alternative therapies and led me along this path, for which I am eternally grateful.

We met each week or two for several years. In the beginning there was an urgency about our conversations. What are you trying now? Which health practitioners are you seeing? Which medications or supplements are working for you? But as time went by, as we each sensed positive change, we allowed ourselves to relax and have more fun with our exchanges. It was a fascinating time with much personal growth and subsequent improvement in my overall health.

Jasmine was (and continues to be) such a blessing, in many ways. She is truly an Earth Angel. When we met, I had been chronically sick for six years without significant progress. Jasmine was still in her first year of illness, but just like me, she had also encountered no helpful solutions within the conventional Western medicine model. We were both offered pills and very little hope. She was quicker to embrace the idea of self-responsibility and exploring complementary therapies, most of which I had never heard of.

The best part about my new friend, though, was that she 'got me'! At last I had someone who walked in my shoes and understood my pain and frustration. It was a great relief to not feel so alone. Perhaps, if you open yourself up to the idea of finding a 'healing buddy', your journey will also become a little easier to navigate – and even fun.

Jasmine and I both made it through to the other side of our Chronic Fatigue, and found a 'new normal' with many new skills and a greatly altered perspective on life. We accessed many similar resources, but eventually forged our own paths by following what resonated most and brought us the greatest results. Jasmine moved on to emotional healing via Tapping and became a highly-skilled practitioner in Faster EFT, a simple and effective holistic stress release technique. It is another natural avenue you may choose to look into. My own focus was more on gut health and nutrition, as well as meditation and energy healing to balance the body and mind; these are what I now teach people when they turn to me for help.

ENERGY HEALING/REIKI (INNER JOURNEY)

There are many paths to the mountaintop (although once there, the view is the same) and we need to select our own way. Perhaps we are all destined to arrive there once we are ready to do the work. Work on ourselves that is – and not just physically. Success requires an inner journey of cleansing and balancing, and is a process of acceptance, forgiveness, embracing gratitude, and so on.

True healing is only possible through changing one's perspective. As we 'rewrite' our life's story, our pain and suffering take on new meaning and actually promote personal growth and transformation. This evokes a complete restructuring of the way we do things and how we express ourselves, as we become unique expressions of our own souls.

In 2010, Jasmine and I started to study an energy healing modality called Reiki. This was quite a leap of faith for me, but it felt like a very positive move. I trusted our teacher, Rosalie, as we had been attending a meditation group that she facilitated, and this had already been helpful and enlightening. Essentially, Reiki channels life force energy through the body to balance and revitalise the systems. It is a simple yet effective form of healing that is delivered through the practitioner's hands on or above the body. It is available to everyone and works on mental, emotional and physical levels, resetting and supporting the body to heal itself.

We have multiple energy centres called chakras, that are aligned with our body systems and emotions. Reiki healing brings them to balance and harmony so that we can function optimally.

Initially, I thought I might just use it on myself and perhaps our dog, but after the first level of training, and practising on family, I was excited by the results and started to see myself working with it. It proved to be a mostly intuitive process, which was ideal for me at that time. I didn't have to stretch my aching brain to diagnose or prescribe treatment (as had been the case throughout my extensive career in physiotherapy) and with my constant head pain, which made thinking difficult, that was a great relief. The training was actually a lot of fun. The mystery of what might be possible excited me, as missing links began to fall into place.

Reiki opened up a whole new world for me, and I was delighted to become attuned at the highest level of Reiki Master/Teacher within the next year. I loved doing the case studies, and was in awe of the amazing feedback from clients. Clients would lie on my treatment bed and I would address any ailments they had listed. It was like a deep relaxation session with the added benefit of aligning and replenishing their energy and shifting the blocks underlying their symptoms. They would report back a few times over the following week with a review of their response to the issues. I could also tune in to friends in other parts of the world and send remote healing to influence their symptoms.

On my first attempt at long-distance healing, a contact who lived interstate volunteered, and we scheduled an evening session. As I sat quietly to tune in to her energy, I wondered what I was doing wrong, as all I could feel was swirling in my head; a quite nauseating dizziness. When I contacted her after the session, she informed me she had been in a car accident that day and was indeed feeling dizzy from her whiplash. It all felt quite magical.

After my initial Reiki training, my dear husband gave me a precious gift by becoming attuned to Reiki energy himself. This was way out of his comfort zone, but as my 'practice buddy' he had experienced the energy in a profound way. He wanted to help me, too, as I still had a constant headache and many other symptoms. This was certainly a gift that keeps on giving. Even today, we can share this beautiful energy with one another in times of need. It is a great blessing and feels absolutely divine.

During this journey, the biggest surprise was how my intuitive abilities opened up. I started to receive information via my psychic senses. Sometimes a client's loved one, who had passed, would make their presence felt during a session. They would give me a name or sometimes even a scent so my client would know who they were. This was always well received by the recipient, and I learned to trust and fully disclose what came to me. Even if it made no sense at all to me, it was often very important to the person I was working with. It all happened organically, and truly fascinated me.

I was keen to explore more possibilities, so I attended a

psychic development group, which was a lot of fun and full of revelations. The group's leader, Lynley, was a gifted psychic and patient teacher. She walked us through many fun activities, like divination (with a pendulum), psychometry (reading energy from a piece of jewellery), and even reading tea leaves. We even did a remote viewing, which was mind blowing. I sat with someone whose home I had never seen or entered, and by connecting with her energy, I was able to 'see' (with my eyes closed) inside her home, describing the layout, furniture and even pets – which she confirmed to be accurate. I was pretty impressed and wanted more!

I also went on to study Seichim, another form of energy healing that proved to compliment Reiki very well. As these energies blended in my sessions, they grew in their power and effectiveness. These days, my healing sessions are highly intuitive. I follow my instincts about where on the body I need to work and move my hands around to channel the energy accordingly. I tend to feel, in my own body, the part of my client that I need to go to next (such as knees, head, or heart). It may sound odd, but that's just how it works for me.

Psychic messages often come to me as I work with the body and the auric field (the energy surrounding a person). These messages include strategies that will help that person move forward without the same problems recurring. Moving beyond what I was used to in healthcare, I found myself using a different term for the people I was assisting. I no longer wished to call them my 'patients' and preferred the term 'clients' instead. I see this as a nod to their self-responsibility. We are a team in their healing process. I am simply a willing conduit and catalyst. My physiotherapy skills and the energy healing aspects blended seamlessly to effectively address underlying causes of multiple issues.

Crystals, oracle cards and even colour therapy made their way into my personal healing path and subsequently the sessions in which I assist others. Colour was a subtle one, but I recognise it now. We are all drawn to different colours, aren't we? And it can change from day to day. Each colour carries a unique frequency, and I believe we are attracted to what we need.

When I set up the 'Healing Space' in my home, I went out to buy a cosy blanket for the treatment table. I brought home a lovely purple one, but as soon as I brought it into that room, it felt completely wrong! I swapped it for a soothing turquoise, which became my colour of healing and hope. Now as I look at what that colour represents, it all makes sense. Turquoise connects you to your feelings and intuition. It builds confidence, improves communication and awakens your heart to your life purpose. Turquoise can help you find peace in difficult situations, as it calms nerves and relieves stress. It makes ancient wisdom available and can provide a sense of connection to your inner mastery. How perfect! No wonder it is my colour.

The year 2011 proved to be a very big year, and probably the first I had faced with optimism since getting sick eight years earlier. After completing the second level of my Reiki studies, someone gifted me an executive pass to a conference in Brisbane called 'Happiness and Its Causes'.

I was terrified at the thought of going interstate on my own. My health still wasn't great, and my confidence had taken a huge hit. I had been relying heavily on my husband for day-to-day support. But, I felt this to be an amazing opportunity, and not an accident. On some level I knew that it was exactly what I needed, so off I went. My resolve was tested on day one, when our airport was closed by a gigantic volcanic ash cloud, and I missed the first presentation! But after that, it proved to be a spectacular experience on many levels. I had so many signs of support from spirit, and I never felt scared or alone.

Thanks to my thoughtful daughter-in-law, I was lucky enough to be at the conference as a guest of the wonderful Maggie Beer, who was one of the speakers that year. I was sitting quite close to the stage and rubbing shoulders with lots of people whose work I admired.

When His Holiness the Dalai Lama came onto the stage, I was overwhelmed by tears of gratitude and joy to simply be in his presence. I had lunch with the beautiful Sarah Wilson of *I Quit Sugar* fame and discovered that we had a great deal in common, especially in the history of our health challenges and what they had led us to learn. I had dinner with David Gillespie, who is also a great researcher and author in the field of health. I had read his first book, *Sweet Poison*, and have gone on to follow other very relevant topics he has tackled too.

In the audience, I got chatting to the lovely lady next to me, who was fascinated by my story. I learned that she was a publisher of self-help books, and she was even kind enough to send me one she thought I would enjoy. *Live the Life you Long for* by Annie Evans addressed many subjects that were dear to my heart, and resonated deeply. I had no thoughts of writing my own book at this stage; I was still trying to get well. But perhaps a seed was sown that day.

It was all quite surreal, but again I knew that there are no coincidences. The Universe was definitely steering me along a better path.

Early in 2011, my diary entries took on a more hopeful tone: 'My health has certainly turned a corner and I look forward to the year ahead. As long as I approach each day with love in my heart, finding joy in each moment and kindness for everyone, things are much better. I sense that I am being transformed, as if there's no turning back now. I even see the daily challenges of life as gifts (in unusual wrapping paper). They are opportunities to learn and grow. And I feel joy in the smallest blessings.'

At this point, I was introduced to another new concept when I met the lovely Cindy-Lee, a medical intuitive. Her advice was tremendously helpful and arrived when I needed it the most. We became 'pen pals' for quite some time and have since become firm friends. Her ability to tune in to my body's needs astounded me, and often my spirit guides would send beautiful messages of support through her as well. The angels were very keen for me to know they were helping, and dear Cindy-Lee could hear them before I realised I could! This in time led me to listen for myself and begin to hear them and record their advice. Little did I know where this was all leading me...

The 'mysterious' phenomenon of Oneness (which I knew little about at the time but came to understand deeply) was another unexpected blessing to enter my life. Jasmine told me she was attending some Oneness groups, then one day she suddenly announced that she was going to India to visit the Oneness temple. To say I was shocked is an understatement. Jasmine, like me, was still not well, so how could she do this? I was worried that a cult or suchlike had taken her in (my own fears raising their head), and I had to find out for myself. I needed to be sure that my dear friend would be safe.

So, off I went to a Oneness gathering with Jasmine one evening, and the rest, as they say, is history. That night I experienced a most gentle and loving, yet powerfully transformative energy, unlike any I had known before. I discovered that Oneness is not a path to follow; it connects you with your own true path. I was completely enchanted and wanted to learn how to share this 'Oneness blessing' (hands-on healing also known as Deeksha) with others as soon as possible.

Before long, I attended a two-day 'Awakening to Oneness' course, which was facilitated by a lovely lady called Janette who had been involved in this field for several years and been to India many times. I was excited to become a Oneness blessing giver and share this beautiful energy of spiritual awakening and transformation with others. Little did I know, it would involve much personal healing and insight. It turned out to be one of the best things I have ever done.

I will never forget waking, on the second day, from a dream in which a white dove (symbol of peace and love) came to me and kissed me on the lips! Can you imagine how that felt? I knew right then that I was on the right path with Oneness. This was further confirmed a little later, when I was doing some yoga stretches on the back lawn before going back to class. I was full of gratitude for all that I was learning and how it would help others, and a white bird flew silently right over my head, leaving me in awe.

I'm not even sure how it happened, but before long, I too was bitten by the India bug! I just knew I had to go there. The idea of doing a course at the spiritual university there, and visiting the magnificent temple, suddenly took root in my mind and very swiftly came to fruition. From the moment I set the intention, everything seemed to fall rapidly into place. It all happened so effortlessly that I'm sure it was meant to be.

So, in February 2015 I took another big leap of faith and embarked on my two-week pilgrimage to India. It felt like a magical mystery tour, and an important next step for me. India proved to be an eye opening and self-empowering journey on many levels. The initial culture shock was far more confronting than I had witnessed anywhere else in the world, as I was thrust into the chaotic traffic, the colourful crowds and pungent smells that are India. And the immense divide between the rich and the poor.

The courses offered at the Oneness University address the inner world, in order to find solutions in the external world. The course I selected was called 'Freedom' – its intent being to connect us with our heart wisdom and higher intelligence, thus enabling us to experience freedom from suffering created in the mind.

Topics covered were Fulfilment, Transformation, Freedom and Awakening. This university, though, was less about receiving information, and more about being immersed in experiences. We were living and feeling what was taught, rather than just acquiring knowledge. I have heard this called 'experiential learning', which has always been my own preferred way of education. This was not an academic pursuit. It felt more like life training and a gaining of wisdom as well as inner strength. It was very grounded and yet mystical. I felt like I had one foot in both worlds, and I loved it!

In Chennai, it was wonderful to meet up with my young friend Albert, and my roommate Rochele. A few of us from Adelaide had decided to do the same course, so that was comforting. On arrival at the university campus, we were greeted with a refreshing drink of coconut water (still in the coconut!), and a red dot was placed on our foreheads with the intent to shield unwanted thoughts from coming in.

There were two hundred of us attending this course! I met lots of lovely people who had travelled from all over the UK, USA, New Zealand, Iran, Germany, China and Japan, as well as other parts of Australia. We were indeed quite a melting pot of nations, divinely united in a like-hearted common purpose.

Processing us through to our accommodation took a very long time. The wheels turn slowly in India, it seems; it's as if time takes on another dimension. The unfamiliar pace was already part of the lesson in patience as we waited to each be assigned a number on a security tag. Hours later, when my turn eventually came, I was surprised and somewhat puzzled to be given number ONE, and the Indian people told me that it was very auspicious for me to receive this. There were many signs like this along the way, leading and reassuring me, and letting me know that I was indeed on the right path.

Ravens seemed to be around me everywhere since arriving in India, frequently getting my attention. There were even two sitting on top of the 'Welcome' sign at the entrance of the Temple on my first trip there. I now discover them as spirit guides: Ravens create change by overcoming obstacles, and their soul mission is to nudge people towards enlightenment. Wow, how appropriate!

Our accommodation was clean and comfortable, and the grounds were very beautiful. I was enthralled by the large number of dragonflies in the gardens, as these creatures had already become very special to me, as symbols of hope and transformation. Indigenous Australian folklore says that the dragonfly, as a divine messenger, embodies the regenerative powers of transformation, urging us to break through the self-imposed limitations that hinder our development and growth. No wonder the dragonflies kept coming close to me and grabbing my attention. I was ready.

Each day at the campus began with a rooftop yoga session at sunrise. I was in Heaven. The shared meals were thoughtfully prepared and wonderfully fragrant, and I will never forget just how extra-delicious the bananas were. Being locally grown and picked when ripe makes such a difference, but I imagine they were infused with love as well.

The energy I felt from the dasas (monks) who taught us was extremely powerful and took a bit of adjusting to. Dasa is a Sanskrit word meaning 'devotee' or 'servant of God'. On the first morning of lectures, I felt quite nauseated, dizzy and unable to concentrate. They reassured me that my body was simply reacting to the higher energy frequencies that were coming in, and it would settle down. It was an intense reaction, but thankfully short lived. I rested for a couple of hours in the afternoon and was fine after that.

I will try to highlight some of the aspects of the course for you, although many parts of my experience were beyond words. We explored the notion that life is energy that wants to flow, and the external world reflects our inner world. All pain and suffering has physical and mental components, and anger and other emotions can arise from resistance. The dasas spoke a lot about relationships – how everyone wants to be happy, healthy and successful, but as human beings we get hurt, and we hurt others. An unhappy person creates an unhappy world. 'Hurt people hurt people.' We are all aware of examples of this, aren't we? Fortunately, happiness also spreads.

When we are prepared to do the inner work and set right our relationships, we can heal the inner child that has been hurt. This can lead us to more peace of mind, greater clarity of thought, optimism and self-esteem, and subsequently better health. We may reach a point where we realise that the hurts we have carried were largely of our own discernment, and we are able to release them. Suffering is never in the fact; it is always in the perception. For example, our parents love us as much as they can, but our fears can block us from experiencing their love fully (as I had found). Equally, their ability to express love to us is largely shaped by their own experience.

We humans tend to hang on to psychological pain for a long time. We work very hard to apportion blame, even hatred, toward people we feel have hurt us. If left alone, it will eventually heal, but we won't let it go. We keep digging up the past and making someone else the reason for our pain, even if only in our mind. This only prolongs our suffering.

Guilt, for example, is an emotion that springs from a remorseful awareness that you have done something wrong. It is a destructive energy that can drain you and make you very weak. Luckily, life offers us freshness in every moment, and opportunities to learn and grow. When we surrender and allow ourselves to 'be' with our emotions, we stop searching for answers outside of our self (which the mind always tries to do). Life becomes more vibrant and energetic again. We can more fully experience the pleasures of life. When you are truly living, as opposed to just existing, you will draw like-hearted people into your life.

As for success, it cannot be defined, yet the fear of failure often holds us back. Our mind makes assumptions and convinces us that we will fail, triggering fear and prompting us to 'run away' from situations. The truth, as they say, is, 'You can run but you can't hide.' The fear will follow you. We are always fearful of uncertainty, although nothing in this creation is permanent. Everything is changing all the time, but the mind does not let us see this. The unknown equates to infinite possibilities (or true freedom). Death is one example. In an ironic twist of life, once your fear of 'losing the known' dissolves, everything in the world can flow well for you. Life is a continuous process of learning, growing and evolution. As we grow spiritually, our consciousness rises and our joy magnifies.

We had many opportunities to meditate while in India. Although as human beings we are all searching for peace of mind, we were reminded that the nature of the mind is to go on talking. It will compare and judge and express a lot of desires. 'Silencing the mind is like trying to empty the Amazon with a bucket!' they told us. The imagery of this impossible task made us laugh. So, rather than change the mind, perhaps we could observe and make friends with it. Our annoying patterns and programs can be seen, on one hand, as contaminating our consciousness, but when all is said and done, they are exactly what makes us human.

We were immersed in many 'processes' during our stay. The dasas meditated, chanted or played music as we did focused breath work and followed along. They led us on some very mystical adventures, which were long and gruelling at times, but always wonderful! I will keep most of the details close to my heart, as they were deeply personal to me, but I can tell you that it was the most intense experience of energy I have had. There were a lot of tears and even some 'ugly crying' as emotional pain was released. But there were also many joyful moments, and some very energetic happy dancing.

The Oneness temple (now known as Ekam) is magnificent and quite magical. Built entirely from white marble, on the principles of sacred geometry, it was such a blessing to be able to sit within this sacred space. I had heard that the temple is home to a field of universal consciousness, an energy imprint that can bring about awakening. I felt very humbled as I first approached, and at that moment a butterfly joined me, triggering a huge emotional tearful release. I was so full of gratitude for being there, and for everything that had previously occurred in my life to make it possible – including my prolonged illness. I was excited to begin my next chapter and overwhelmed by the opportunities that continued to appear.

Soon after the 'awakening' process we experienced within the temple, the number 447 started appearing to me repeatedly. It was even on the number plate of the bus I returned to campus on, and I saw this number another three times within the next hour. This felt highly significant, and on checking the Angel Numbers (Joanne Sacred Scribes website), I found that '447 is a message of praise from your angels as you have been working diligently on your soul mission and they are most pleased with your progress.' What a beautiful confirmation for me, and another reminder to remain open to the guidance that can cross our paths in such unexpected and creative ways.

The ultimate aim of the course was to lead us to become spiritual masters within our own lives, making a real impact on others and thus on the collective consciousness. By taking what we learned and grounding our spiritual growth and expansion into the physical reality of our lives, we would be able to lead by example and stand as a lighthouse. As we ensure that the energies we project are loving and uplifting, our presence can be a healing force for others. When we find our way out of the low vibration of our limitations, we create a pathway that others can follow, thereby assisting humanity and the evolution of our beautiful Earth.

It would not be possible for me to quantify the effect that my trip to India had on me, my family or those around me, but I am confident that it was a positive influence. It felt a bit like an energy upgrade, and I can certainly look back in awe at the direction my life has taken since then. Many people who have attended my meditation circles or sought my energy healing work have also reported and displayed significant benefit. We may not be aware at the time, but everything happens for a reason, doesn't it?

PART THREE

NEW BEGINNINGS AND WELCOME SURPRISES

CHAPTER 9

Make Peace with Your Past (Acceptance, Forgiveness and Gratitude)

'THERE IS NO NEED FOR TEMPLES, NO NEED FOR COMPLICATED PHILOSOPHIES. MY HEART AND MY BRAIN ARE MY TEMPLES; MY PHILOSOPHY IS KINDNESS.' **– HH DALAI LAMA**

I did not have an unhappy childhood, but I never felt quite 'good enough'. I was the second girl, when I'm sure Mum and Dad would have loved a boy, and I always felt that my big sister was the smart one. I tried to live up to very high standards. If I came second in the class, my dad (bless him) wanted to know where I went wrong. I seemed to be on the receiving end of more criticism than encouragement or praise, and this made me anxious to please, which became an ongoing fruitless quest. It may have been a construct of my mind, but I felt somewhat insignificant, too, as if my voice never mattered. I was prone to allow others to undermine me and repress my point of view.

I must have grown up very fast. Don't get me wrong. I was loved and nurtured and well cared for, but like many of us, I grappled with my self-confidence and self-esteem. I am also a natural redhead, which in those days was more ridiculed than revered, and I unfortunately allowed the opinions of others to affect me a great deal. One of my dad's friends laughed at me one day by the pool. He said that redheads like me think we have a suntan when our freckles get bigger and join up. He probably didn't mean to be cruel, but it was a touchy subject for me. I was deeply hurt and have never forgotten.

In more recent years, I started to feel an urgency about improving my relationship with my father. Although I loved him dearly, I knew that I was not relaxed in his presence. We didn't engage in much meaningful conversation, and I often failed to show him the real me. I always reverted to my inner child, who felt that what she had to say would be judged as trivial, or not heard at all. Dad was approaching eighty and was not in the best of health, and it felt to me as though time was running out. I wanted to be able to talk to him and share with him; involve him more in my life. But even as a grown woman, I was afraid! How sad is that.

I eventually became aware that my fear was in no way logical; these were my issues, and the way to improve things was to work on me! I had to recognise and release the limiting beliefs that were no longer serving me. I meditated, prayed and called in my angels to help. I started to connect with my inner wisdom, open my heart (to myself and everyone else) and allow my soul to lead me forward. This worked brilliantly.

I was amazed and delighted at the recognition and response from my dad once I stopped holding back. It became very clear that he loved and respected me; he simply didn't know how to say it or show it in the way I thought I needed. Our relationship flourished and I began to enjoy our interactions. In time, Dad started to talk with me more openly. One day he surprised me by sharing that his (dear departed) mother had visited in the night, and he had felt her sit on his bed! He seemed quite happy about this; we weren't so different after all!

Keeping a part of me hidden had been harming me and my relationships. What we hide about ourselves keeps us distant from others and the world. It was very freeing to realise this, and very rewarding to find the courage to make changes.

It still surprises me that I have become a spiritual teacher. Others saw it coming, but not me! It makes me think of Rumi's teaching about the wound being the place light can enter. I'm sure I would not have travelled this path without the impetus of my dire health. What a mountain I had to climb, but something made me keep going. Perhaps on some level I knew it would be worth it and the silver linings would be many.

Centuries ago, the philosopher Socrates said, 'To really know thyself is the beginning of wisdom,' and Plato wrote, 'All learning is simply recollection.' While study can be helpful, all we truly need to know is inside us. We can come back to our innate patterns of pure perfection, even when the mind forgets. My own 'rock bottom' point led me on a spiritual quest to know myself better and share what I discovered.

I have since heard it said that fulfilling your soul's purpose is learning to be happy right where you are, no matter how much better things are destined to become. I love this! When grace enters our life, it is a mystical force that soothes us in subtle ways; it will often come to us as inspirational thoughts.

In May 2015, having returned from India and taken some quiet time to process my amazing adventure, I started to feel an urge to share my writing and blog about what I had learned. Perhaps it was all a precursor to birthing this book:

BLOG

'THE POWER OF GRATITUDE'

'Good morning. This is my very first blog post. I have to admit that I am a little unsure of myself in tackling this new project, but here I am, taking that first step into something that I have felt brewing for a while. So here goes . . .

In my Healing Space, I have a bowl of gratitude marbles. It reminds me every day of all the things I have to be thankful for. I see my cup overflowing and I count my blessings. The idea for my gratitude marbles came to me during a meditation circle several years ago when I was just embarking upon my path of spiritual awakening.

I remember being very excited, and couldn't wait to get home from the group and fill up a vessel with something abundant. Rose petals perhaps? And then I found the colourful glass marbles that I had apparently kept since my children were small. I had completely forgotten that we still had them, but the symbolism felt perfect, as they immediately reminded me of how lucky I am to have my beautiful son and daughter and the families that they are now forging. I set the marbles up in a lovely chalice in a prominent spot where I could enjoy and be inspired by them.

The very next day, I was walking on the beach as usual, collecting sea glass as I do, and there, grabbing my attention in the sand, was a gorgeous, weathered glass marble! Turquoise blue glass, roughened by the sand. I couldn't believe my eyes. I felt so happy and grateful, and knew it was a clear sign that I was on the right path. I took it home and added it to my bowl, where it still lives with my other gratitude marbles. I often pick up broken glass of all colours, shapes and sizes on my beach, but I have never seen another sea glass marble, and I don't know anyone who has!

This may have been the first time I consciously acted upon an inspiration, and it was immediately reinforced. I was in awe of the power of my guidance from the unseen world, and gaining great hope for the future.

Being in a state of gratitude holds tremendous value, as it has such a high vibration. On a personal level, it always led me back toward a place of inner peace, even though I was in the midst of a debilitating chronic illness.

We are powerful co-creators of our life experience when we learn to work in harmony with the universe. The spiritual Law of Attraction dictates that if we want to change what or who we attract, the best way is to hold more loving and joyful thoughts. We can repel or magnify situations as we choose, so these days I try to remember to visualise and affirm only what I desire.

I'm sure you've heard the adage 'Energy flows where our attention goes'. In other words, we always get more of what we are thinking about, whether we want it or not! It is always a good time to elevate your thoughts to a more positive level and higher frequency.

Several years ago, I read an inspiring book called *365 Thank Yous*, by John Kralik. It was about how a man changed his life with gratitude. He wrote a thank you note to someone every day for a year, and what he gained from it was amazing. I was inspired to send some notes too. I wrote to some of the prominent people in my life who had been supportive and kind. I handwrote the notes on lovely stationery, with my heartfelt words of gratitude. I was unattached to the outcome and really enjoyed the experience; it made me feel happy. And then something amazing happened...

On a wintry day, I was walking along the esplanade toward the post box to mail my first few thank you notes – and there, in the middle of the muddy path, was my favourite hat. Now why is that so incredible? Well, my hat had been missing for more than a month. It was a gift from my daughter-in-law when we were visiting Paris, and I was very sad to think I may have lost it. I used the soft animal-print beret to cover my ears from the wind on my morning beach walks. One day I realised I had dropped it, but there was no sign of it when I diligently retraced my steps. Now, on this auspicious day almost five weeks later, I nearly stepped on it! It was clean and right side up despite the wet conditions, on a path that I had trodden many times since losing it. I was speechless and delighted. A gift from the angels – who knows? It really felt like a reward for the healing work I was doing on myself. I couldn't stop smiling for days.

So, my suggestion is to take every opportunity to say thank you. Invoking genuine gratitude – the kind you feel, not just say – creates a very high vibration in the heart, giving a sense of deep satisfaction. To live in a state of gratitude may just be the greatest gift you can receive. Of course, love and gratitude go hand in hand. The more grateful we are, the more love comes in, and love is the most powerful and positive force in the Universe.'

***

Early in 2016, I suffered a significant loss with the passing of my dear old dad. It was a long and tedious process for him and the family as his health progressively failed. After six weeks in hospital for acute care, we had to move him and my mum into an aged care facility and poor Dad passed away only five days later.

My father had been Mum's carer for several years, holding things together since her memory had started to fail, and he was very worried about leaving her behind. I'm sure he dug in very deep and hung on just long enough to get Mum settled into a new home. He knew that there, she would get the care she needed. Dad was also very aware that their bond was so strong Mum would never have left the family home without him. What an amazing soul. Even the nursing staff were in awe of his Herculean effort.

In the last few weeks of Dad's life, he said lots of things that surprised me and made me proud. It actually appeared to us that he was a changed man. Faced with ongoing hospitalisation, multiple surgical interventions and the prospect of never returning to his home, he amazed us with his attitude. He was full of praise for the doctors and other staff, incredibly patient with Mum's incessant questions, and outspokenly grateful for all the work behind the scenes, especially to my sister and me.

When told that no more could be done for him, that he would have only palliative care and most likely bleed to death over the next few days, Dad shed tears that were rarely seen. Still, he was incredibly compassionate for everyone else. He even mentioned how difficult it must have been for the specialist to tell him that. His acceptance, compliance and tenacity were astonishing. He had survived numerous risky surgeries and bounced back from death's door many times, but his main concern was always for Mum, who had relied upon him so heavily.

Despite the grim prognosis, we all found his care to be exceptional and I witnessed lots of little 'miracles' along the way. Even Dad acknowledged that there was a force bigger than us all at play. He told me it felt as though everything was being orchestrated. This realisation was a great relief to him, I think. We teased him that he must have been 'touched by an angel' on one of his near-death experiences, which amused him greatly, but he didn't share more about that I'm sad to say. What I witnessed was a man who had always tried to tightly control everything let go of the reins and allow life to flow and unfold. An enduring example to us all.

The emotional wound I felt on losing Dad was very deep, but I am glad that I was able to appreciate many blessings as well. For example, the quality of the care we encountered, the love and support of family and friends, and the close bond I developed with my sister. In this time, we formed a strong team and achieved a great deal for our beloved parents.

I am so glad I trusted my intuition and made the effort with my father. By the time he passed away, with Mum and me by his side, I can truly say that I had reached a point of immense gratitude and compassion for him. I miss him terribly, but now remember him with only unconditional love, gratitude and respect. Dad has even found ways to contact me and talk about his life on the 'other side'. How differently he sees things now, and how proud he is of us all!

Mum continued to live in the aged care home, so it was necessary to pack up their things and sell their house. This was an incredibly difficult process for me, yet also quite cathartic. I didn't like making decisions on their behalf, and Mum was only able to keep a very small number of their possessions in her tiny new space.

My sister and I kept a few meaningful items for ourselves and our family and donated the rest to those in greater need. The very first item I came across when packing was a silver pendant of my dad's. It has a set of scales on the front (Dad was a Libra) with the inscription 'Everlasting love from Carol and Ian' on the back. I sat on the floor and dissolved into tears!

My husband and I had bought this for Dad in Switzerland on our overseas trip in 1979 and I had forgotten all about it. So had Dad, I suspect. How amazing and perfect that the very first trinket box I opened in his study held something that connected Dad to me. I wear it every day now, to feel close to Dad and to remind me about keeping balance in my life. I'm sure Dad is pretty happy about that, too.

One night during this packing process, I was meditating in the bath and I suddenly knew that I needed to start writing this book. In my mind's eye, I saw myself in one of our spare bedrooms, but it was converted to a writing room with a long desk and my dad's bookcase! There were even notes all over the walls outlining the chapters. My story needed to be documented in order to help others I 'heard'. It was like a download, and somewhat of an epiphany.

Inspirations often come to me in the bath or shower, when my mind is given a chance to settle. These were very clear and I knew I needed to act upon them as soon as possible. So, we moved out the bed and cleared the space, and Dad's big bookcase came home to my place. My husband asked me several times if I was very sure that I wanted it, as he knew it would prove to be a quite difficult piece of furniture to transport, and he was certainly right!

But, I couldn't deny what I had been shown. I remained adamant, so home it came. It felt very right in my room, filled with many old books, a few of Mum and Dad's ornaments and a recent photograph of my father. The desk I had visualised also materialised in double quick time – the very next day, I noticed that a friend was selling it online for a nominal amount, and I was able to collect it right away. Our son then very kindly brought me a computer and screen that his office no longer required. And my daughter-in-law, who is a talented writer and very clever with tech, gave me lots of welcome tips on getting started. The icing on the cake was when we won the raffle on Grandparents' Day at school – and we were able to bring home a very cheerful painting of a rainbow, which was done by our eldest grandson and his six-year-old classmates. We hung it right behind my writing desk, where it continues to uplift and inspire me every day.

In 2017, my mother passed away quite suddenly, just a year after Dad. They had been married for sixty-five years and I have no doubt she died of a broken heart. It struck me that, as an empath, I had been feeling Mum's pain too. She had her world turned upside down in an instant, losing her husband and her home within a few days. Even though we had frequent lovely visits with her and took her out on excursions as often as possible, I still felt guilty that she had lived out her final days in a nursing facility with 'strangers'.

My logical brain knew that this was where she needed to be, and it was in fact a wonderful place with amazing staff, but it still never felt quite right to me. Now that Mum was gone, I was bereft. How do you say goodbye to the first person who ever loved you, who always held you and told you everything would be OK? Somehow, I found the strength to speak at her funeral, buoyed up by the strong feeling that her story deserved to be heard. I did the best I could, and I know she would have appreciated it.

I discovered that loss could bring many emotions to the surface. I tried to allow them all, while learning to forgive myself, again. Mum had lived much of her adult life in fear of getting Alzheimer's disease. Her own mother had dementia from quite a young age, and many other family members followed suit. Mum also lived with resentment and regret from childhood, as her parents would never reveal to her the identity of her biological father. Despite our research, Mum went to her grave not knowing, but his identity was surprisingly made known to me, long after Mum died. I'm sure they have since met up in spirit and all is forgiven.

As I learned more and more about the metaphysical aspects of disease, I came to understand the power of our thoughts and emotions. At times I had been judgmental and frustrated by the choices Mum made. It is so hard to watch loved ones suffer, especially when you have the tools to help them. But we must of course allow their own free will, no matter what. It is their chosen path, and everything is always in divine order, after all.

My grief was overwhelming at times, and I had to pull back from life and be gentle with myself. I was very reluctant to step into the role of the matriarch. They were big shoes to fill, but my lovely Mum would be proud. I must say, though, I am pleased and somewhat surprised by how well I have stood up to this tumultuous time of major life changes and deep grief.

Against the odds, the tools that I have learned to employ in recent years have acted in good stead and kept me balanced and well. I no longer deny my emotions; I allow myself to feel them fully. I also tune in regularly to what my soul needs, and I try to action this. Music, for example, has been very healing for me. I currently play Mum's funeral songs over and over. But it's not a morbid obsession. On the contrary, these songs were selected with loving care and carry great meaning, and they truly help to soothe my soul.

Quite often, my soul craves more stillness and silence. I want to retreat and hibernate like a bear into a cave. To BE instead of DO! But I am also feeling a firm hand on my back, encouraging me to do more. To experience more, achieve more and share more. Do you ever feel like you are too busy, but also not busy enough? I sometimes grapple with this and strive to find the balance.

The Universe is showing me the way forward, creating opportunities for my personal growth and supporting me to step into the fullness of who I am and the life path that my soul has chosen. I feel this at a deep level and know that it is true. I put a lot of pressure on myself to 'get it right', and I feel a greater sense of urgency now that I have reached . . . a certain maturity, shall we say? But time is just an illusion. I have to keep bringing my attention back to here and now, this moment, the only one we have. I ask and tune in to my inner being, 'How am I feeling now? What do I need right now?' I am acutely aware that we must honour the answers.

A few years ago, we were visiting Sally and her family in New Zealand. We always try to have a mother and daughter outing of some kind when I am there, and Sally usually has a plan for something nice like a massage or movie. But this time, her idea really challenged me: 'I think we should get a tattoo together.'

I didn't see that coming! In my six decades on Earth, I can honestly say that I had never considered getting a tattoo. My first response was very resistant. I started to make up all sorts of reasons why it wasn't going to happen, and for the next two days I kept saying NO. But there was a battle going on inside of me. On one level, I liked the idea. It felt somewhat rebellious and playful. But there was also fear (the emotion that commonly holds us back). I had no idea what I would choose if I went ahead, and where on my body would it go?

What on earth was I afraid of? When I walked the nearby paddocks for hours to tune in, I realised I feared being judged. Really, at my age? My parents were in spirit, so their disapproval was no longer an issue. Oh, but there was also fear of 'getting it wrong' (that's a big one for many of us) and all the 'what ifs'! What if I chose the wrong symbol and regretted it later, or what if the tattooist didn't do a good job and I didn't like it? It was a fascinating process to observe.

I gradually opened my heart to the idea. I didn't want to disappoint my daughter, but I knew I should only go ahead if it was right for me. I felt into the possibility of getting my first tattoo at age sixty-two. I kept walking and started to notice dandelions everywhere. My son-in-law, the farmer, didn't think this was a good choice. He sees them as annoying weeds, but I was very attracted to them! (I love how he respects my point of view, and affectionately calls me Yoda.) When I researched the symbolism, it was perfect. I saw some lovely drawings of their seed pods, and eventually decided to do it! I added two small birds to the design to symbolise my mum and dad flying up to heaven, and I chose to put it above my wrist, where I can see it. After all that, I have never had a minute of regret. In fact, I wear it proudly and it makes me smile.

Tattoos are seen by some as contrary to the direction I had taken for my body and health but I considered all of the risks (like skin infections or allergic reactions to the ink). And, when I silenced the negative committee in my head, logical decision or not, it FELT right for me at that time. It was a leap of faith for sure, but sometimes that is exactly what we need.

The dandelion carries symbolism that is centuries old. It is the symbol of a free-spirited soul, and of hope and resilience. As a pillar of strength, it reminds us that we are able to survive anything, bounce back from adversity and continue to grow. Weeds to some, perhaps, but how perfect for me!

Turmoil only arises when the mind runs away. The balance, of course, lies within. When I align with my heart, breathe deeply and listen, I can access the wisdom of my eternal Self – the part of me that knows all and never leads me astray. All I have to do is connect my head with my heart, and the thoughts transform. They nurture my highest benefit and no longer cause me stress.

Time in contemplation – simply 'being' – is never wasted. When we allow this or indeed embrace it, the 'doing' side of life takes on more meaning and clarity, and it flows with greater ease and grace.

Human beings are complicated – you might say we are a bio-spiritual ecology. The best 'medicine' is therefore always individualised. There is no 'one size fits all'. But once you are conscious of better choices, there is no going back. It can feel like a big responsibility when we first discover all the work involved in reclaiming our power, but once the inner knowing becomes loud enough, you can't ignore it.

Sometimes our desire to produce a certain outcome can cause the rational mind to go in the wrong direction, but I have learned that we can always trust our feelings. I call this Emotional Intelligence. An ongoing 'bad feeling' is probably the voice of reason, and a clear guideline that your proposed plan is not the best way to proceed! I can recall many personal experiences of this, some of them quite dramatic. Smart people listen to those feelings, and the most intelligent among us cannot learn and grow without harnessing the power of intuition. I have noticed that beauty and joy elude those who try to manipulate their life. You cannot change the course of a river – it must go to the ocean!

Yes, it takes time and effort, but the payoff for your health is tremendous. We can only go forward. We can't go back and we had better not stay stuck or conflicted. The relentless calling of my soul, and the support of my beloved family and friends, have seen me through this, given me strength and solace, and allowed me to give birth to what you now hold in your hands. May my example inspire you, my friend, to bring forth your own shining story.

CHAPTER 10

Angels and Miracles (More Than Meets the Eye!)

'THE SOUL ALWAYS KNOWS WHAT TO DO TO HEAL ITSELF. THE CHALLENGE IS TO SILENCE THE MIND.' **– CAROLINE MYSS**

You may recall me saying that I had always been a science and facts kind of girl. But, in my ultimate quest to find my own answers and get myself well, I discovered many other dimensions. I have been guided and supported by inexplicable forces: what I now call 'the invisible reality'.

Even as I write this, it feels a bit like I am 'revealing myself' as an angel lover. It can be intimidating to share our personal beliefs, but perhaps owning my connection to other realms will encourage you to explore your own . . .

My first angel encounter was in 2009, at a weekend retreat in the countryside. I was fifty-four years old. I was learning new concepts for healing, like forgiveness and gratitude, and I was loving it. At one of the tea breaks, I stood alone in the garden, enjoying the serenity, when a small white feather fluttered down from the sky and landed at my feet. There were no birds or trees in sight, and there was no breeze. Although it seemed illogical, I just KNEW that my guardian angel was helping me. I put the feather in my pocket and couldn't stop smiling. My connection with and love for the angels, and how we in fact help one another, has continued to grow. I still find white feathers frequently – often in unexpected places.

I also found that significant numbers started to appear to me, like 1111 and 444. They would repeatedly grab my attention, glaring out at me from things like car number plates, clocks, addresses and phone numbers wherever I went. As I researched the symbolism of each number, its meaning would always hold a relevant message for me at that time. And this was just the beginning.

Oh my goodness, I kid you not! The word count on my computer just caught my eye, and there's a 444 in there! My angels are beside me right now and happy that I am writing. I love it when they remind me.

Birds and other creatures have also appeared as messengers at various times in my life, sometimes in completely obvious ways like coming into my house! When I research their symbolic meaning, they always carry some helpful spiritual guidance. The following are some of these experiences that I have journaled.

In May 2011, I had just completed a weekend course in the city, and had some experiences that shook up my emotions. On the long drive home I became very upset and started to cry. I knew it wasn't a good idea to drive while emotional, and I had a long way to go, so I called in some help. I silently asked, 'Please stop my tears so that I can drive home safely.' A white car pulled out right in front of me. It had a 333 number plate, which immediately made me feel safe, happy and grateful. It led me for several kilometres, and I was feeling much better by the time it turned off again. According to the Angel Numbers website, the number '333 tells you that the Ascended Masters are near you. They have responded to your prayers and wish to assist you.' Holy smoke, how amazed I was! (By the way, Ascended Masters are spiritually enlightened beings who dwell in higher dimensions but have been human in past incarnations.)

In June 2011, I visited my mum and dad for an hour and was about to leave when parrots started to chatter furiously near my car. It somehow felt significant, so I sat in my car for a few minutes just absorbing their sounds. When I drove on to collect my husband from his office, I came across a serious four-car collision that had just happened in my lane. I felt that I had been diverted from disaster and gave thanks. I'm sure the birds had kept me from harm's way. Spirit indeed works in mysterious ways.

I have read that the message from parrots as spirit guides is about delving into the past to heal the inner child. They also ask us to speak with positive, supportive and encouraging words, remembering that we have the power to influence others with lasting impact. This was so very relevant to my relationship with my parents at that time. Spot on again thank you!

I have had many close encounters with the beautiful dragonfly, but this one takes the cake. In December 2013, on the morning of my daughter's wedding in New Zealand, all the 'girls' were together having our hair and makeup done. Sally's wedding dress was hanging from the rafters, and her shoes and jewellery were all laid out ready for the big event. We watched in amazement as a large dragonfly flew into the room, passed close by us, then slowly circled the room as if checking out all the beautiful things before flying right by us again! Sally and I were sure this was a sign from her grandma, my lovely mother-in-law who had passed two years before. Our family had meant the world to her, and she was making her presence known. What a great blessing that she was with us for the special occasion.

Through my spiritual journey, I have come to believe that we do not disappear when we die. Science tells us that energy cannot be destroyed, only transformed, and that we are energy. The infinite part of us that many call the 'soul' continues on. We are still able to feel our loved ones around us and communicate with them, albeit in a different way.

Many of my psychic senses started to elevate when I became Reiki attuned. I was connecting with something greater than intuition now! I wasn't drawn to practice mediumship as such, but when working with clients I would sometimes sense a fragrance or hear a name that I needed to pass on to them. It wouldn't always make sense to me, but it was often very comforting and healing to them. So, I learned to trust what comes to me and always fully disclose it to whomever I am with.

Early in 2012, I was doing an energy healing session for a woman in need, from my home office Healing Space. It was a very significant session with lots of healing from her past, especially long-held childhood pain regarding her deceased mother. As we finished and she got up from the treatment bed, I hugged her and found myself saying, 'I love you, Celeste.' I had never said this to a client before. She cried and cried and told me, 'My mum never ever said that to me.' Well, I think she found a way to say it that day. How wonderfully heart-warming for them both. And for me, of course, to realise that spirit could speak through me in this way.

In June 2013, my friend Marcia asked me to host a new meditation circle in my local area, using the Oneness blessings (Deeksha) that I had been attuned to share. I was so nervous and unsure about it, and yet accepted the challenge without hesitation. This was so unlike me.

In the little back room at her lovely crystal shop one Tuesday afternoon, twelve people arrived. We could barely fit all the chairs. There were lots of people I didn't know. One lady said she was guided there. Another brought her dog along and told us the amazing story about how she and the dog had been rescued by dolphins. There was a psychic ten-year-old boy who had asked his mum if they could attend the group. Even my own daughter was there, on a 'surprise' visit home from New Zealand.

It was a very beautiful gathering, and I was overwhelmed with tears of gratitude as I listened to them introduce themselves. It certainly diffused my nerves and made me realise that the group was very needed and 'meant to be'. This group continued almost every week for seven years and was held in my Healing Space until Covid. People continued to come and go as needed. It was such an honour to witness their personal growth as they moved through their own challenges with greater ease and grace, stepping into their true selves.

Awareness of the eternal nature of the spirit helped a great deal when my parents passed away. The grief is still very real, and the process must be allowed, but being open to spirit enabled me to cope, and to receive little messages and signs. The number of times the 'Hello from Heaven' card has flown out of the deck as I shuffle my oracle cards is amazing! It always makes me smile and remember that whatever is going on in my life, I am not alone. I would love to share one beautiful experience from last year that also highlighted this . . .

A few months after my father passed away, Ian was scheduled to have knee replacement surgery. (I know! So much trouble with his joints, poor guy.) It was to happen in the same hospital Dad had been in for six weeks, where I had visited him every day. I was feeling rather stressed and alone as we went to town for the pre-operative appointments. We stopped for morning tea in the café opposite the hospital, and when I looked up, there sitting at a table directly opposite me, reading the paper, was my dad!

My tears flowed uncontrollably as I gazed at him, and it was doing my head in. It wasn't like seeing a man who looked a bit like my dad, it was like looking at my dad. Every detail – his hair, reading glasses, shirt colour and so on. I took a sneaky photo and when I look at it now, it is still 'my dad'. As I tried to process it all, I felt that it was a strong message of support, letting me know that I was not alone. I sent the photo off to my kids, who were just as blown away. My daughter even said, 'That's grandpa, you should go and give him a hug.' Fortunately, he left the café before I had a chance to act on that impulse. Imagine how freaky it would have been for him.

When I found the courage to show my mum the photograph a few weeks later, she agreed that it certainly appeared to be dad. At that point, she decided she would like to visit a medium to try to hear from Dad, and it turned out to be a lovely experience for us both. Dad had a lot to say. He made it abundantly clear he was still around us both, aware of our current situations, and sending beautiful signs of support – such as the monarch butterflies that started to appear around me soon after his passing.

The following year, my husband unfortunately had to have another big operation! As we waited to see the anaesthetist, we were chatting about the doctor and wondered what his first name was. As he came out to greet us, he shook my hand firmly, looked me in the eye and said, 'Hi, I'm Kenneth.' I literally took a step backwards and held my breath – that was my dad's name! I knew then that my husband was in good hands.

When my mum passed away only two weeks after this, her carers reported that she had recently started to 'see' Dad and talk to him. He was around to comfort us all. How wonderful is that?

I have started to hear guidance when I sit and listen. I like to write it down as I go. Sometimes I feel that it is not just for me, so I share it online – and when I do, I often get feedback that someone needed to hear it that day. Here is one example that came through recently . . .

BLOG

'A MESSAGE FROM THE ANGELS'

'Dear ones, we are near you. Your beautiful souls make our hearts sing. We your angels are so thrilled that you are setting aside more time to connect – not only with us but with your own true selves.

For when you align with the vibration of love and peace within your own heart, the world changes. This small act of being still, allowing the mind to settle and remembering more of who you are, is invaluable. And the ripple effect is immense.

Never underestimate your power. When your heart is open and your intent is pure, miracles can manifest. Not in ways that your human thinking may imagine, perhaps, but miracles, nonetheless. Be open to our love. Welcome it into your being. Follow the guidance that comes from this, and you will be pleasantly surprised where your life will take you.

Take some moments to set your goals, create your vision and establish a plan. Put your intention clearly forth, then step back and allow it to unfold. Action steps will be required when inspiration strikes, but most importantly, retreat and surrender to the process. Get out of the way so that the magic can happen.

This means bringing your thoughts back to the present and raising your vibration through self-care and prayer. We are always ready to hear you and draw near. Just ASK!'

***

I love the simple but clear wisdom that comes through when the mind settles, and I aim to tap into this at some stage every day. I encourage you to be still and listen also. As we quiet the mind, there is opportunity to connect with new information and inspiration. When I forget to ask the angels for help, they are quick to remind me in creative ways. For example, I often see relevant words on number plates, and 'ASK' was the first one to appear. It is still my most frequently noted word. Angels are always ready to help us but they will not contravene our free will unless asked (apart from in life-threatening situations)! So remember to call on them.

Around this time, my husband and I attended a party with many of my new 'spiritual friends'. The conversation got around to angels, and my normally quiet hubby spoke up to everyone about his beliefs. I was stunned at the realisation that this wonderful man, who I had been married to for thirty-five years, had believed in angels his whole life. How could it be that I had only just discovered this?

This was a pivotal moment for us as a couple. It opened so much great new conversation; we sat up all night talking. I had many tears of gratitude in knowing how my life partner fully supported the spiritual growth that was opening for me. I didn't have to be shy about any of my new experiences – he was very keen to hear everything about them. Having a loving sounding board right next to me has made an enormous difference.

Soon after this, Ian and I attended the funeral of a friend who was our age and taken by cancer. We talked a lot about how we felt and discovered that our attitude toward death had evolved. We were very sad, especially for those left behind, but we had much stronger acceptance, and comfort within the knowledge that the spirit goes on. These realisations had come at just the right time for me; they proved to be an even greater blessing a few months later, when my dear mother-in-law passed away unexpectedly.

Oh, another word count moment, right at 35,555 as I glanced down. That is a lot of fives, and in numerology, fives are all about change! This certainly was a time of massive change for us. My husband's mother was the first parent we had lost, and her sudden passing (although this was the way she would have wished it, I'm sure), left us all reeling in disbelief. We miss her terribly and her passing affected me deeply. I am thrilled, however, that she has found ways to communicate with us from beyond the veil. Our connection continues on.

After the Oneness workshop and my trip to India, I attended a workshop about angels. I started to feel a strong connection with them and wanted to learn more. We meditated and I made my first attempt at 'automatic writing'. Trying to trust what I was hearing, I intuitively wrote a question at the start, and found that the answers poured forth onto the page, which surprised and delighted me.

Here are the words I scribed:

'How Did I Heal?'

I started at a place that felt like rock bottom.

I thought I was going to die, and that it would be a relief to die! This frightened me and gave me the impetus to go on, to not give up, to find the answers.

Conventional medicine was not the answer, but the answers lay inside of ME.

I learned about the mind-body connection,
how what I think determines what I feel.

I learned to FORGIVE and what a great gift this is.

I learned to get in touch with my Higher Self, my inner wisdom,
and that when I am quiet in body and mind,
I find clarity and peace within.

I learned that spirituality is the essence of life.
I learned to be a warm-hearted person,
and I learned to keep on learning.

I learned that everyone does the best they can with what they
have at any given moment.

I learned that I don't have to control,
in fact it is better to surrender.

I learned that life is simple, only we complicate it.

I learned to be grateful for every moment, every experience.

I learned to be ME.'

This, my very first experience of channelling wisdom onto paper, completely amazed me. I was fascinated by how easily those words flowed, and to this day they are very relevant and helpful. For many years, each day I wrote the guidance I heard in a notebook. In more recent times, the angels have encouraged me to speak the words out loud, as this 'voice channelling' carries a healing vibration along with its transmission.

There is a lovely French proverb that designates patience and perseverance. It translates as: 'Little by little, the bird makes its nest.' For a long time, I felt like the little bird, as I opened up to more aspects of myself step by step.

As you know, I became very accustomed to creatures showing up as messengers – which was likely why the bird proverb connected with me so well. Yet, in 2016, I was very surprised when I met 'my horse'. Each week, my husband and I drove about forty minutes along country roads to visit my mum in her aged care facility. There was a more direct route, but we rather enjoyed the scenic 'back roads', and one day I saw a beautiful pale-grey horse at a property along the way.

He initially caught my eye as he was leaning against a shed, which seemed a very cute and unusual pose. I noticed him almost every time we drove past, and before long I found myself looking forward to seeing him, hoping to spot him. When I did, he always made me smile. He was always alone in different parts of the same paddock. I even had a crazy thought, which took me by surprise, about how much he resembled a unicorn.

One week before Christmas, my husband and I were chatting while driving home and realised that we had driven past the horse's field without seeing him. Something drew me back. We turned around and drove to his paddock, where my husband pulled the car over for the very first time. This beautiful horse was at the back of his enclosure, but as I opened my window, he locked eyes with me and came straight over to the fence.

I got out and went to him, wading through long grass, and he allowed me to pat him. We looked into each other's eyes, and I can only describe our meeting as a reunion. It felt like I knew him, and I was so full of emotion. I could not stop the tears from flowing. There was so much love between us. It was like reconnecting, and I didn't want to leave him!

He nuzzled and licked my arm, and I hugged him as I wept. I had an apple in the car, so I fed that to him and he accepted it with delight. We hung out for a few more minutes before I dragged myself away, stunned and amazed at this inexplicably beautiful encounter. It was such a surprise to me how drawn to him I was.

I love all animals but have not had much to do with horses in my life. As a child I had a couple of quite frightening experiences – being thrown from one horse, and kicked in the back by another. Yet I had no fear of this animal. There was only love and magnetism between us, a strong demonstration of heart-to-heart connection.

As I pondered this powerful experience later, I checked my reference book. In *Animal Dreaming*, Scott Alexander King states: 'Horse is a symbol of personal power, and a spiritual journey within in search of inherent wisdom, unleashing a world of unlimited potential, maturity and enhancement on all levels.' This felt so right for my current state of personal growth and expansion. It was amazing confirmation that we had met for a reason.

I have continued to visit 'my horse' whenever I can, although we don't have cause to travel in that direction very often now. I met the owners a few months ago and found out that 'he' is actually a twelve-year-old female called Skye. She always gallops over to me as soon as I pull up, although these days Skye seems more interested in munching the apples and carrots I bring her than accepting the pats and cuddles. Still, she always brings me joy.

My guides tell me this horse was by my side in many lifetimes, a loyal companion and wise soul in her own right. I think I may have had the privilege that day of meeting one of my spirit guides in person. She certainly helped me to navigate a very challenging time in my life, full of grief and other emotions. Life continues to fascinate and delight me at every twist and turn!

Meanwhile, our neighbours had a pet chicken their kids called Bok-Bok. We loved hearing her happy noises when she was laying. At one point she decided she wanted to come and live in our yard. I was wary of her at first, but soon grew to enjoy her visits very much. She would even roost in a tall tree right outside our upstairs kitchen window. At dusk we watched her flutter and climb her way up high and settle in for the night.

After some time, I overcame my fear of being pecked or scratched, and realised she was very gentle and looking for some loving. I would sit on the grass with her and she would climb into my lap for cuddles, which always felt wonderful.

When I explored the spiritual meaning of chickens, the main message was also one of heart connection. According to Spirit-Animals.com, 'Chicken is asking you to take some time for inner evaluation. Scratch the surface of your emotions and see what lies underneath.' Soon after this, she was gone. She had served her purpose and moved on, as our messengers often do when we have received and understood their guidance. I felt very blessed to have connected with her. Thank you so much, Bok-Bok!

If you encounter chickens along your path, perhaps ask yourself, 'Am I responding from my heart to the circumstances around me?' There is always something to be acknowledged.

CHAPTER 11

Be Well with Me
(New Beginnings and Endless Possibilities)

'THE SECRET OF CHANGE IS TO FOCUS ALL OF YOUR ENERGY, NOT ON FIGHTING THE OLD, BUT ON BUILDING THE NEW.'
- DAN MILLMAN

Here I sit, happy, healthy and whole. I have reflected on all that has brought me to this point in my life. Now, I can share with you the way wonderful things can be born from the depths of despair.

I knew from the outset that this final chapter would be chapter eleven. It just felt right. No coincidence there, as the number eleven symbolises new beginnings. The single digits side-by-side represent the upright posts of the doorway you and I are about to walk through. The final chapter of this book is, of course, only the beginning of a new chapter – for me and for you!

I also felt called to write the last chapter first! I really had to document my happy ending before immersing in the pain and suffering and hardship that I would need to revisit. And I'm so glad I did!

My journey has not been easy, but it has taught me a great deal, and I am truly grateful for it all. I was once leading a blinkered life, but the Universe had other plans for me. From that watershed moment when I thought it would be a relief to die, my life has opened up immensely. I have learned how we can integrate the head and heart to relax the analytical brain and connect with the trustworthy guidance that lives within us.

Our instincts become sharpest when we need them most – when we are navigating turbulence. The more we follow our intuition, the more doors will open to help us fulfil our life purpose. For so long, I did not recognise the innate spiritual gifts and resources within my own heart and mind. I repeatedly gave away my personal power. It was such a great feeling to take back the reins. Ignorance is certainly NOT bliss!

Have you noticed that when you discover a purpose in your life, you seem to step into a magical flow? It can be like entering a different realm, where the Universe rearranges things to fulfil your deepest desires. Synchronicities seem to align, bringing your way the people and other resources you need.

Looking back on my 'former' life, during the ten years of my chronic illness, it was like driving through thick fog. I was unable to see where I was going or enjoy the experience. And always on high alert. There can still be some bumps in the road, but the fog has well and truly lifted. I can navigate life with clarity and awareness, and even enjoy the ride.

Most of my days are now spent in pursuits I enjoy. Meditation, yoga, energy healing, gardening, beach walks and writing are some of the activities that nurture me and build my equilibrium. And, of course, interacting with my four precious grandchildren as often as possible. Children are so great at keeping us focused on the present moment and reminding us to have fun.

I still meet a range of emotions and some of them can be pretty uncomfortable – such is the human experience. I am sometimes happy, sometimes sad, but deep down, there is a fundamental strength at my core. Emotions are a barometer of our life experience, so I allow myself to feel them fully. I have let go of judgment (of myself and others) and embraced tolerance and acceptance. I am so glad I can see the bigger picture now, from a higher perspective. It brings me great peace. Not right away, maybe, but always in perfect timing.

As I write today, my heart is very full. I feel so blessed that I have lived to dance at my son and daughter's weddings, and to welcome my fabulous grandchildren into my family. Life is so precious and joyful again.

My daughter, her husband and their two little boys live in New Zealand. We visit them as often as we can, but they have a dairy farm and can rarely get away. In the past two weeks, they have been here with us for the first time in three years! We are fortunate to have our son and his family only an hour away. So, this has been a very joyful time, surrounded by all of our family, watching the young ones play together and get to know their cousins in person. This mother hen has felt so happy to have all her eggs in one basket.

Today, when the overseas contingent left to travel back home, I experienced the deep sadness, tears and heartache that come when it is time to part. However, I am more able to focus on the positives than I used to be. I can still smile as I recall the fun we shared together . . . and all the fabulous hugs! I am grateful that my family took the time out to reconnect, and I am getting better at accepting the physical distance between us (even though I will never like it!). When I take a step back from the logical mind, I can sense our heart connection that transcends all time and space.

This is just one example of the peace I believe comes from a deep sense that everything is exactly as it should be. It is not a logical process, it is a 'knowing'. No matter what is going on in my life, I am sure there is a powerful force much greater than me driving things forward in a positive direction. I am certainly not in charge, and I don't need to be. I feel a great sense of comfort and relief when I remember that.

An excerpt from my most recent blog may serve as a summary of what has led me back to my strong sense of self . . .

BLOG

'YOUR MOMENT OF TRUTH'

'How do we know if we are living the life that we came here to experience? This is not something you can answer with your brain, as the mind will make up all sorts of stories. It is definitely something, however, that you do know in your heart.

The key is to quiet the mind for long enough to hear the truth of your soul; that ancient, infinite, consistent part of you, which has been your essence since the beginning. Some like to call it the Higher Self, and this term resonates with me. I believe it is the spiritual part of us that is never ending and wise beyond measure. The part of us that is always connected to our original Source and knows all the answers we seek. The part we can trust, that will never let us down.

When making important decisions or life choices, how do we know what to do? Imagine that there is a 'fork in the road'. Which is the correct path for us? Should we toss a coin, or follow our intuition? What if we ask our Higher Self? What if the choice has already been made for us, and we just need to 'remember' or step into it. How can we know?

Trust your feelings as your reliable inner compass. Compare the choices in front of you but not with your mind. See yourself making the first choice. FEEL what it is like to be living that choice and note the emotion attached to it. Is it a positive or negative feeling? Then imagine yourself living the life of the other option, and FEEL how that sits with you, the emotion it evokes.

Is it expansive, easier to breathe, or constrictive and tight in your gut? Does it make your heart sing – or sink?

Both choices may feel 'OK' but only one will feel 'right'. Don't second guess yourself. Nobody knows better than you. Trust your inner guidance, for your instincts will never let you down.

Now, of course, 'knowing' is just the beginning. Even if you trust your feelings, nothing will change unless you take action. You must step into your Truth. It may feel like a leap of faith, but don't worry. No one can ever feel prepared for momentous change. And know this – the bigger the need to pursue this path, and the greater your soul purpose is, the more your ego will try to talk you out of it. The ego (personality self) does not like change, and it may throw up doubt and fear and judgment and a host of curly questions.

Try to recognise this chatter in your head for what it is. Step aside to be the observer; allow it to pass and don't buy into it. Keep sinking into the energy of your heart space. Be still and hear your wise old soul. Its message will be positive, clear and repetitive until you really get it!

You will learn to love and trust your Higher Self. You will find more strength and beauty there than you ever imagined. This is a journey of the inner world. A connection with yourself that you may have denied or perhaps even feared. But only love and truth exist there, and the wisdom of your soul.

Communing with your higher wisdom always brings you into the present moment, the here and now of this very existence. And the present moment is the only place where we can truly experience love and healing. It is all we have, and we must cherish it.

There is nothing to fear about learning to love and trust yourself more. In fact, it may open a whole new world for you. You may learn a lot about what 'makes you tick', find a new sense of purpose, or even accept yourself fully for the first time. It's a great feeling, as if all the pieces are falling into place. A new sense of pride and belonging that is very nurturing. Criticism and judgment fall away, and self-belief flourishes. You are ready to do what you want, what you NEED. You can let go of all the conditioning and surpass the 'shoulds' and 'musts' you have accumulated along the way.

You know now that it is only right when it FEELS right. Intuition can be very powerful. We have all heard stories of it saving lives. So trust your instinct, your gut feeling and inner voice. It can be accurate guidance about the path ahead. Tune in to it often and it will become even clearer. Your stress melts away as you connect with this 'knowing'. It brings you to a warm and fuzzy place where you feel strong, and you feel LOVED. The outside world stands still, just for a moment – this moment, your moment, the moment of Truth.'

***

I now know, in my heart, that everything will be OK. All is exactly as it is meant to be, divinely orchestrated for the highest benefit of myself and those around me. We are not victims! Life is not happening to us; it is happening through us and for us. This inner knowing enables me to navigate my way through human challenges, to witness from a higher perspective while allowing my feelings to arise. The more I know and trust, the simpler it becomes.

Author Katherine MacKennet once said, 'Every time I witness a strong person, I want to know: What dark did you conquer in your story? Mountains do not rise without earthquakes.' I feel this way too. I am aware that the long and varied – and at times, very tangled – web of my life has been a magnificent tapestry. It is an ongoing work of art that I now cherish every part of.

Indeed, I LOVE my life! And I certainly have not always been able to say that. Most importantly, I love and fully accept my SELF (most of the time).

Life is never dull, but change is inevitable and welcome. There is so much to experience, to learn and grow from. For example, relationships teach us a lot about ourselves, don't they? How you react to people is always about what is going on inside of YOU!

It is very empowering to know we have complete control over ourselves (and NONE over anyone else!). I don't mean 'control' in any manipulative sense. I mean that we are responsible for our own thoughts, words and actions. There is no one else to point the finger of blame at; it is all up to you.

If that sounds scary, don't let it be. Self-responsibility is actually a wonderfully expansive concept. Once you realise your health and happiness are not in anyone else's hands, you will begin to step into your authentic life. There is no point in judgment, blame or excuses, and no-one is coming to rescue you! Retrieve the parts of yourself that have been abandoned or lost and need some tender care. You are not a victim of your circumstances. You can create and respond to your world at the same time.

There may be deep-seated beliefs and patterns of behaviour that you have inherited or absorbed, but it is still your choice whether you activate them. How cool is that? You really are the creator of your own destiny, a master manifest-or! You can choose to steer your life in a more positive direction. You can truly write your own story, not only retrospectively as I am doing, but in the here and now, one choice at a time. There is more to your story than you have ever let yourself believe.

There are many and varied emotions, but in essence they all fall into one of two categories. Either they make you feel GOOD, or they make you feel BAD. This doesn't mean they are right or wrong. You simply like the way they feel, or you don't. I choose to engage with 'better-feeling' thoughts as often as possible.

I liken this to the field of epigenetics, an aspect of health that continues to intrigue me. People with health challenges are often diagnosed with inherited 'damaged genes' and told that this predisposes them to a myriad of symptoms and disease. But most modern-day disease is metabolic – related to our diet and lifestyle choices.

You may have a predisposition to a family ailment, but you no longer need to believe that you will get heart disease just because your father did, or dementia because your mother had it! In most cases, our genes are not our destiny.

In fact, research has shown that our diet and lifestyle choices actually regulate our genes. They express them (switch on) or suppress them (switch off). We can constantly change and renew the components of the body. Just like our unwanted thoughts, which we can choose not to engage with, it is quite possible to have 'damaged genes' and choose not to activate them. Trust that things are never what they seem. Life is working for you.

Similarly, we don't have to erase our old memories or beliefs. We can simply learn how to not have them active, or not be under their influence. They are like old programs that we can displace or supersede. Try to remember the best things from your life, and not give too much attention to things that may not be going so well. This takes practice, but is well worth the effort, as it raises your vibration and aligns your precious energy in a very beneficial way.

So, make better choices. You have the power to be WELL.

Often, our self-condemning thoughts and beliefs erode our spirit. They steal away our sense of self love, peace and joy. Even our life force. It doesn't have to be this way.

Life is a journey away from fear, and back to love, as humanity gradually moves from the 'love of power' to the 'power of love'. Life has a way of bringing our attention back to what we need to be present with. Everything that arises is real, valid and likely to be leading you somewhere greater. It is all energy in motion, and we must allow it to move through.

Think of a beautiful gorge like the Grand Canyon. Over time, the massive erosion has created something spectacular. Should we resist what is happening and try to get back to where we were?

No. Let us surrender to what we are becoming and settle in to enjoy the ride.

I am excited when I see science meeting spirituality in our world. We are all such a fascinating blend of both. The heart is where the body and spirit come together to make us human. From our hearts, we can face our fears, heal our wounds, and acknowledge that we need to remember who we truly are! Then, we gradually recognise everything that is ego-centred and find ourselves in the vibration of the heart. We become peaceful, happy to be ourselves and able to face whatever life brings, with love and compassion for all.

With integration of head and heart, we start to live with wisdom, in the knowing that we are all eternal spiritual beings having a human experience. I know. This is 'big'! Don't try to get your head around it; you will just know when you know. It is an ongoing process. Be patient with yourself. I am thankful for my awareness and deep connection to the Earth. Nature is my sanctuary.

In recent times, I took my notebook on my morning walk and felt the need to be still and write.

'Today as I sit on the wet sand, gazing out to sea, I am completely at peace. This was certainly not always the case, but now, I am aware that I have so much to be grateful for.

I have to admit that I used to be a profound overthinker. I would always get ahead of myself with the 'what ifs' and I thought that I had to control life. I recall a very close friend bringing this to my attention once, and I became quite defensive. I gave him the whole 'It's just who I am and I can't change that!' speech. Thankfully, I have learned better now.

Now I can pause here and quiet my mind. I listen to the waves lapping at the shore, I smell the ocean and feel the sand between my toes. I watch the hooded plovers flitting side to side, and I am fully present in this moment. Tension, tiredness and worry from recent events melt away and allow me to connect with my heart, the centre of my being, where my loving soul resides.'

I am proud of who I am and how far I have come. My heart still hurts at times – with the physical distance that separates us from loved ones, for example – but I am much less inclined to buy into Earthly dramas. Despite the inevitable onslaught of global disaster and tragedy, there is a peace and tranquillity at my core that I have never had before. I feel deep compassion for these situations, but I can find my way back to my centre. Being able to tap into this, and guidance from higher realms of consciousness, is such a blessing. I remain positive and optimistic as much as possible, with my heart open and always aligned with my purpose. And I am grateful for each new day I greet!

We are all navigating a mind, body, and spirit maze, and there are many ways to the centre. Developing greater trust and faith in the Self, one choice at a time, eventually leads to trust and faith in something far greater. There is not only hope for the future, there is hope for a better, brighter future. It's a hero's journey and the hero is you. If I can survive what I went through and have a great life, so can you. Please don't ever give up!

Know that you are not your thoughts or the voice of your mind! You are the consciousness that listens and is in each and every cell of your body. Step back from the mind chatter and become the observer of your thoughts, feelings and physical body. Trust your innate intelligence; the part of your consciousness that remains in the quantum field. This is what operates your body moment by moment, overseeing all the chemical reactions that are happening within your trillions of cells. Your innate intelligence communicates with your DNA, cells and organs. The inner landscape is always informing the outer landscape. As you start to identify with the energy of your consciousness rather than the thoughts of the mind, you will find that you are able to connect with the wisdom of this other aspect of yourself.

Every choice you make will create a consequence. Do not align with fear, or your choices will be made from a fearful place. Recognise fear as the paper tiger and move into a place that brings you peace. You have all the tools that you need. True healing is about evolution, letting go of attachment to the personality and surrendering to the higher intelligence of the body. Inviting your profound mystical inner authority to co-create your life.

Believe in the power of love and its positive influence on yourself and others. It is time to shine your light, dear ones. Set it free and beam it out. Transform, within yourself, to be the change you wish to see in the world. We are in an era of profound global transformation. We are all feeling things we've never felt before, so we must act responsibly and participate with wise choices. One person can really make a difference!

Can you view each day as the first day of the rest of your life? This is my approach as I strive to be the best ME I can be. It all starts right here. With you and your willingness to learn, grow and be fully present. If we are not moving forward, we are stagnating, so I suggest you embrace your opportunities as they appear. Say YES, and then work out how! No one was ever fully prepared for anything momentous (didn't someone famous once say that?), so don't let your doubts or fears hold you back.

Once you 'know', there is no going back. Yet being conscious of better choices can feel like a big responsibility. Especially when you know you have to do the inner work in order to take back your power. It does take effort. However, each day is a clean slate, an opportunity to start over. There is no point in beating yourself up about yesterday! Live for the moment. Do what you can, when you can. No regrets. Just live with purpose, every day.

What do you really want from life? Deep down, you DO have the answers to this question. You may have forgotten, but they reside deep within your being. It's all about the path you forged before you came here, for a lifetime of living, loving and learning.

So, dear reader, I hope you can now see the immense value in nurturing your connection with your Self. I have demonstrated, through my own life experience, what it is like to be fearful and lost, but also how it is possible to find your way back to self-love and self-healing. Who would have thought that my many years of chronic illness would present me with so many wonderful adventures, and lead me to the extraordinary life I now have? So much inner peace and clarity has come with this new way of being, which simply involves being true to myself and my soul purpose, moment by moment!

The life of contentment that we all strive for is only ever a deep breath away. Pause for a moment and place your hand on your heart. Doesn't that feel better already? You are feeling your connection to the real you, your eternal essence or soul Self. The peace and wisdom this brings forth will reassure and uplift you, every time you need it. In an instant.

The trick is remembering to not go down the rabbit hole of stressful thoughts. As with establishing any new habit, this takes commitment and perseverance, but the payoff will be magnificent. You will be kinder to yourself and everyone else. And you will be heard and appreciated in far greater ways.

It is time to be true to the potential that lies within you.

My last words of advice are these: the night is always darkest before the dawn, so don't quit five minutes before the miracle! Keep track of how you are feeling and trust your emotions to guide you. Work at feeling GOOD about the things that really matter to you, and watch as your health flourishes, your dreams unfold and you step into a life of purpose, prosperity and joy. A life you will LOVE . . .

PART FOUR

RESOURCES

Ten Top Tips for Healthy Living

Are you looking to rebuild your life after a health crisis? Perhaps it is time to stop avoiding needed and long-overdue changes. Your past mistakes or fears may be holding you back from the healthy choices you have been seeking. You may feel overwhelmed by the magnitude of the task, but please trust that you have nothing to fear and a great deal to gain by taking action now. It is not just your body you are trying to balance, it's your whole being.

Harmony will be restored as you restructure the way you see yourself and how you do things. As you start to believe in yourself, others will no longer undermine you, and healing won't be nearly as difficult as you imagine. All healing is truly self-healing in the end, but there are many tools and resources at your disposal to facilitate the process.

I have detailed my top tips for you in this section. However, they are not laid out as a road map. Start with the steps that resonate with YOU! Notice what you are drawn to. Trust your intuition. You know in your heart what is best for you.

Of course, we must take steps, for without action, we have only great ideas! One step forward at a time – slow and steady wins the race. Be patient with yourself as you establish new habits and learn how to prioritise your time. I hope these resources will help you like they have me. Whatever you choose to do, I invite you to please pursue health and happiness as though your life depends on it... because it really does!

HEALTHY CHOICE 1

QUIET THE MIND

Our thoughts can cause us a great deal of stress, and they are often not even the truth! They keep us in the past or project us into the future. The mind can run away; one thought can become another, and another. We go around in circles replaying stories based on old beliefs or patterns of behaviour that no longer serve us.

Mindfulness brings our attention into the present moment, so we can live in and fully experience the now. Did you know the present moment is the only place where we can truly experience love, happiness and healing?

We cannot stop our thoughts, and we really don't need to. We can learn to step back and observe them, to live less in our heads and be more heart-centred. When we connect our heart with our mind, we establish a perfect resonance, and our thoughts will become more positive and gratitude filled. And we all want that!

You may choose to follow a guided meditation, listen to soothing music or join a regular meditation circle. Some people find it is easier to quiet the mind within the collective energy of a group. You could try to see your thoughts as leaves on a stream floating by, or as words on a conveyor belt. I like to visualise the personality/ego sinking down into the soul to have a little pow-wow, learning from the wisdom there and taking it back to the head. Fear and pain dissolve as love and joy take their place, so it is not so much about what you gain from meditation, but what you can lose!

There is no right or wrong method. These are just some ideas I have gathered, and it is a matter of finding what works best for you. Meditating is certainly not about 'blanking off'. Rather it is allowing ourselves some stillness, to simply BE, with no doing, trying or expectations of any kind.

When we focus on the breath, the heart rate slows. Our physiology responds in many beneficial ways. Don't try to stop your thoughts, rather take a back seat and become the observer. As you are calm and objective, insights may come forth into your awareness.

You can have a special place you go which is your sacred space, or just close your eyes and explore your inner world, wherever you may be. There are even many helpful apps at our fingertips. You may like to sit in nature, or light candles and play peaceful music, but even the shortest retreat from the busyness of your day – with a few deep breaths and a smile – is very beneficial. This is a perfect way to reset. To soothe your nervous system, get out of the stressful 'fight or flight' mode and into the replenishing 'rest and restore' state, which we all need more of.

***

HEALTHY CHOICE 2

BREATHE DEEPLY

Like most people, you may be unwittingly doing shallow breathing for much of the time. This is not ideal. Consider the multiple benefits of drawing air deeply into the base of your lungs.

You will improve your body's oxygen uptake and assist your airways in staying clear. You will feel the benefits of stress relief and enhanced body awareness. Consciously monitoring your breathing could also make you more mindful and heart-centred, getting you out of your head space and allowing you to be more compassionate with yourself.

When your mind is going back over old stories, they can make you feel angry, sad or even depressed. You may feel anxious, because your thoughts are racing ahead to fabricate unlikely possibilities. Bring your focus to the rhythm of the breath, which will anchor you to the here and now. In the present moment, the healing power of the life force can truly work its magic.

Each day, simply sit or stand comfortably and rest your hands on your belly (between your ribs and navel). Consciously engage your diaphragm by breathing deeply. You will feel your tummy rise and expand under your hands as you inhale and shrink back as you exhale. Breathe in for the count of three and out for the count of five. Repeat this pattern five or six times, and try it before bed and before each meal. Notice how you feel more relaxed, centred and calm.

This kind of breath work will even wake up your digestive enzymes, by engaging the 'rest and digest' part of the nervous system. Hence, your gut may be happier too, and that can have lots of additional benefits.

Sadly, air pollution is a modern-day consideration. Even indoors, with the off-gassing of volatile organic compounds from our furniture and floor coverings. Getting back to basics is helpful. Air filters, indoor plants and crystals may all help, as well as good old fresh air. You might like to visit the seaside or green spaces to breathe easier, or simply open your windows.

***

HEALTHY CHOICE 3

DRINK SUFFICIENT WATER

Many people who feel unwell are chronically dehydrated, which majorly impacts basic health. All body systems function better with adequate water intake. As you establish this habit, you are likely to notice an improvement in your skin, digestion, energy levels and more.

Water helps flush toxins through the body, has zero calories, and acts as an appetite suppressant. If you feel like snacking, drink a glass of water and wait twenty minutes. Sometimes hydration is what your body is actually craving, so the urge to eat will subside.

But how much is enough? My easy rule of thumb is to consume about 30mls of water per kilogram of your body weight daily. This equates to a mug full of water (300mls) for each 10kg of your current weight.

Try starting your day with a cup of warm water and the juice of half a lemon. This cleanses the liver and sets up a more alkaline environment for your body. Adding a little raw local honey and grated fresh ginger can also be beneficial, and I find it quite delicious.

If you can, drink water mostly between meals. Water you ingest with a meal dilutes the stomach acid required to adequately digest food, so it may be counter productive.

Drink clean water of the best quality you can access. What does this mean? Consider the age of your water pipes and impurities like heavy metals that may be in your water supply. Read up on various filtration systems and what they're designed to remove. Decide whether you want to consume the fluoride, chlorine or other additives that may be present in your water (that's a 'no' for me!). Or, prioritise spring water, because of its purity and helpful mineral content.

If you haven't yet been drinking water regularly, it may be wise to build up your consumption gradually. Also, try adding a pinch of nutritious salt (pink Himalayan) to your bottle or glass. You won't taste it, and the water uptake by your cells will be enhanced, which means fewer trips to the loo.

Some people don't like to drink a whole glass of water at a time. If this is you, carry a water bottle with you and keep sipping away at it. Keep it close by in your car, handbag or on your desk. You might also fill a jug each morning and place it in a prominent position in your kitchen. This assists memory and motivation, and also helps you keep track of daily intake. Each time you go to make a cup of tea or coffee, make a habit of drinking some water while the kettle boils.

It's important that you don't just drink water in hot weather or when you are thirsty. It deserves your regular attention. In fact, after the age of fifty, we cannot trust the thirst mechanism in our brain to remind us to drink, so we really must make it a habit. Does this sound like something you could easily improve upon?

***

HEALTHY CHOICE 4

REDUCE YOUR TOXIC LOAD

There are many toxic aspects to modern life that we can approach from different angles. We are exposed to thousands of man-made chemicals the body was not designed to deal with. We ingest, inhale and absorb them every day. Some are environmental and largely beyond our control, but many we bring into the home ourselves, so we must learn to make safer choices.

What does DETOX mean to you? Most people are aware of the choices we have with food. They know that it's best to steer away from commercially made and advertised 'convenience' foods. These are highly processed and full of nasty additives that prolong shelf life and keep profits high. They can be very addictive, and our bodies are not designed to deal with them. I can assure you there is nothing convenient about being chronically ill!

Have you thought about your home care and personal care products? The average woman is exposed to over one hundred chemicals before she leaves home in the morning. The good news is that most of the toxins we are exposed to every day are in our homes, brought in by us. You can research and support responsible companies that are doing the right thing by you and the planet. You and your family will thereby avoid a barrage of harmful chemicals that can be endocrine disruptive (affecting our hormones), carcinogenic (cancer causing) or neurotoxic (damaging to the brain and central nervous system).

These chemicals occur frequently in commercial laundry powder, air freshener, toothpaste, shampoo and body wash (even the ones we bathe our babies in), moisturisers, skin care, cosmetics, and the list goes on.

Other modern-day considerations include air pollution and electromagnetic radiation.

When we are loading the body with these foreign substances, we are asking it to continually 'put out fires' instead of giving it the ability to repair and rejuvenate. We certainly can't feel well, energetic and vital. When you learn how to create a healthy home, your body will breathe a sigh of relief. Your blood will be cleaner, your lungs will be clearer, and your liver will thank you, as it won't keep getting clogged up trying to filter your blood. I witness positive benefits every day once people purchase with greater awareness.

Of course, thoughts and emotions can be toxic and damaging to the body too.

**

HEALTHY CHOICE 5

MANAGE YOUR STRESS

We all experience stress in different ways every day. A little bit of stress can keep us 'on the ball', motivated and alert. But in today's world, we are often on overload, which is exhausting and potentially damaging. Cortisol is vital for our metabolism and is released by the adrenal glands as our 'fight or flight' response. However, when our stress hormone levels remain high, our general health is adversely affected.

Perhaps you have experienced adrenal fatigue. Are you exhausted after a good night's sleep, or do you frequently crave sugar and carbs? Years of constant over-activation of the adrenal glands renders them unable to regulate many of our essential hormones. This seems to be the stress syndrome of the 21st century.

Please be aware that stress is not so much about what is going on in your world, but how you choose to respond. If you are feeling stressed every day, you could find that it is impacting your physical body. The root cause of your stress can be a combination of mental, spiritual, emotional or dietary issues.

There are many helpful strategies you can employ. I'm sure you will know best what works for you, but here are some of my stress busting ideas:

- *** AFFIRMATIONS:** positive messages you tell yourself until you believe them. These counteract negative self-chatter and send a better message to the Universe.

* **AROMATHERAPY:** pure essential oils have an immediate effect on the brain. They bypass the intellect and work on the subconscious. Choose therapeutic grade oils to enjoy as a safe alternative to fragrance or perfume.

* **COMMUNITY:** connect regularly with like-hearted people. We all need to feel that we belong. Even when physical distancing is necessary, it does not need to cause social isolation.

* **DEEP BREATHING:** focus on the movement of the chest. It's very soothing and keeps your focus in the present.

* **EARTHING/GROUNDING:** connect your bare feet with the earth (sand, grass or soil). As the trees take our carbon dioxide and give us oxygen, the Earth will take our fear and give us the energy of love.

* **EXERCISE:** walking, cycling, swimming, or whatever movement suits you.

* **GARDENING:** connects you with nature and is very grounding and energising.

* **GRATITUDE:** this raises our vibration and attracts more things to be grateful for.

* **HUGS:** we all need these every day. Embrace each opportunity (pun intended) to give and receive hugs freely. Like me, you may have sorely missed these during pandemic restrictions.

* **MEDITATION:** in any shape or form, alone or in a group, guided or silent. A reliable stress buster, and scientifically proven to have vast health benefits.

* **MINDFULNESS:** give your full attention to the here and now. Don't get ahead of yourself or dwell in the past. Experience this moment fully with all your senses.

* **RELAXATION:** notice any tension in different muscle groups and consciously release.

* **SMILE:** even if you don't feel happy, smiling can trick your body into releasing endorphins (happy hormones).

* **STILLNESS:** find a few moments here and there to just BE.

* **YOGA:** works on body, mind and spirit; a great combination of stretching and breathing, with multiple benefits (outdoors if possible).

If you are overwhelmed by the world, make your world smaller for a while. Stop watching mainstream news or spending time with other challenging energies. Stand in your sovereignty and learn to regulate yourself. Go within and withdraw your focus from external events. Trust your limits and conserve your precious life force.

***

HEALTHY CHOICE 6

EAT REAL FOOD

All too often, we eat for all the wrong reasons: taste, convenience, habit, comfort or cost. Much modern food is high in sugar, salt and fat, and is very addictive. There is no denying a strong link to the epidemic of chronic diseases we now face. Sadly, many of us are overfed and undernourished! Our 'cravings' are likely to be the body asking for micronutrients – even though we may hear 'chocolate or chips'. There are many resources you can consult about specific cravings, i.e., what the body is lacking and suitable food solutions.

Nutrition is at the bedrock of health, so it is always wise to eat cleanly. Choose whole foods that have been nourished by the sun and 'untouched' by man. Eat like a hunter gatherer – meat, fruits, vegetables, nuts and seeds – with a variety of colour on your plate, and especially lots of phytonutrient-rich leafy greens. Grow your own or support growers who do not spray. Explore your local farmers market.

Fresh and local, organic and sustainable is also the ideal way to go. The human body will only be able to fully recognise and utilise food that is not genetically modified, is grown without pesticides and chemical fertilisers, and does not contain artificial ingredients or preservatives.

Educate yourself about healthy fats and minimise your consumption of trans (damaged) fats, processed sugar (especially fructose) and refined starches. Avoiding 'white' foods is also a good rule of thumb – that is, highly processed carbohydrates.

Food labels can be confusing but try to look at the ingredients list and become more aware of what you consume. Move away from processed foods and be cautious of marketing or advertising, which always has a hidden agenda. Limit your intake of additives, preservatives, flavouring (the 'numbers' under ingredients on labels). Trust Mother Nature, not what comes out of a factory or laboratory.

Here's a big hint that will help – don't buy rubbish! If it's not in the pantry, you can't be tempted. But, you don't have to deprive yourself. Start to see your healthier food choices as the ultimate act of self-love, moving you forward in a direction that you desire.

Eat well and your body will reward you with more energy, vitality and mental clarity – at the very least.

***

HEALTHY CHOICE 7

HEAL YOUR GUT

The power of the gut-brain connection is undeniable. My years of constant headache proved to be a case in point. It is crucial to maintain optimal digestion and a healthy gut wall, and to be aware of the host of modern-day challenges where this is concerned.

There are thousands of research papers on Leaky Gut Syndrome. They explain that when the intestinal mucosa is damaged, undigested food particles, toxins and disease-causing microorganisms can breach the gut lining and pass into the bloodstream. This will then trigger white blood cells. This is evident on live blood analysis, which can be a fascinating and enlightening test to have. This situation results in intestinal inflammation, nutritional malabsorption, many skin problems and eventually autoimmune disease. Leaky gut will often result from repeated antibiotic use and has also been found to contribute to liver disease and depression.

Gut dysbiosis is an overgrowth of harmful bacteria, and we need to make sure these are outnumbered by beneficial gut bugs. A prebiotic diet is important; that is, whole foods which encourage the proliferation of a host of healthy bacteria and an intact gut lining. Intestinal integrity can also be adversely affected by many things, for example, unhealthy diet (abundance of processed foods), excessive alcohol, environmental contaminants like heavy metals, repeated use of anti-inflammatory and other prescription medications, and prolonged stress. A quality probiotic supplement can be of great benefit in restoring balance. They certainly work for me.

A healthy gut lining and an abundance of beneficial gut bacteria is crucial to boost the immune system. It can improve your body's blood sugar control, lower LDL cholesterol and fight off infections. Our happy hormones are even made in the gut, so your mood will become more stable.

Let your digestion guide you. Be aware of your bowel habits and whether they are ideal. Do you suffer any digestive upset, such as nausea, heartburn, bloating, indigestion, acid reflux, constipation or diarrhea? None of these are 'normal', and they may be simply addressed by diet and lifestyle choices, with massive ongoing benefits.

***

HEALTHY CHOICE 8

MOVE YOUR BODY

Another way to make your body happy is to walk, so put on comfy shoes and get moving! A 30-40 minute brisk walk is often best for cardiovascular fitness, and 10,000 steps per day is ideal – but don't let that deter you. Any movement you can do will be helpful.

Some of your winter aches and pains may be due to inactivity, as our joints are lubricated by fluid and need motion to distribute this and stay well 'oiled'. Our body's lymph system is like a sewerage system, but unlike the blood, it doesn't have its own pump. When we are idle, toxins are stagnant. Cold hands and feet can be an example of acid waste stored in the extremities. Walking helps to move this waste out of the body.

In fact, walking has endless benefits. It aids digestion, lifts the mood, strengthens the bones, and, if you are connecting to nature at the same time, it warms the heart! Its rhythmical nature can also be quite meditative, quieting the mind to relieve stress, and allowing insights to appear.

Listen to your favourite music or an educational podcast as you walk. Maybe you would prefer to walk with a friend or in a group, as we all need social interaction to boost our mental health. Choose what suits your needs and best fits into your lifestyle.

Start with a 10 minute stroll around the block if that's all you can manage at present, and build up from there. Add more incidental walking into your day as well. Walk to post that letter or purchase the milk. Park your vehicle further away from the shops or the school. Walk with your family to enjoy their undistracted company, while also encouraging physical activity and connection.

If walking is really not your thing, just move your body in whatever ways suit your circumstance and your schedule. If your job is sedentary, consider using a standing station for part of the day (sitting is the new smoking, they say!). Every type of exercise can be beneficial, especially if it promotes balance and strength. If you choose something you enjoy, it is much more likely to be sustainable. Yoga, cycling, swimming and tai chi are all popular pursuits that have multiple benefits (even more if practiced outdoors). You are only limited by your imagination.

Get moving regularly and watch your life change.
Have you had your walk today?

***

HEALTHY CHOICE 9

FORGIVE EVERYONE FOR EVERYTHING (INCLUDING YOURSELF!)

I like to call this 'Radical Forgiveness'!

If you are willing to forgive but still feel the need to judge or condemn, nothing will actually change. When you maintain a belief that someone else has done something bad to you, and as a result they are responsible for the lack of peace and happiness in your own life, you remain in a 'victim consciousness'. You are giving away your power.

However, when we take responsibility for our own choices, such as how we respond to situations and events in our life, we can forgive without the need to blame. Then, everything changes for the better. Forgiveness is a key that opens the heart to infinite possibilities and underpins peace of mind.

Did you know forgiveness is a gift you give yourself? It does not condone or excuse what may have happened. Nor does it mean you have to keep company with the person/s involved. You simply choose to let go of any toxic energy, anger and resentment you are holding within your body. Unburdening in this way is of great benefit to your health and happiness.

Forgiveness is a mystical act of self-healing that defies the logical mind. You must rely on the power of your inner nature, for that is where you can heal. The mind can sometimes make you feel better, but true healing is in the province of the soul, where change can be immediate and profound.

It is said that holding on to unforgiveness is like drinking poison and expecting the other person to die. It cannot work to anyone's advantage. You are only hurting YOU! Let go of all blaming and complaining and watch your life transform. When we speak negative words, we give them more energy. Allow only positive thoughts and expressions to inhabit your sacred space.

And, while you are at it, please be sure to forgive yourself! You are no doubt holding on to numerous self-deprecating emotions. We are so used to automatically taking blame. Find a way to let go of these burdens before they impact on the physical body too.

Speak only kind words to yourself. This is crucial and you deserve it. Trust me, it feels a whole lot better. You may need to recruit some help with this, but please give forgiveness a try!

***

HEALTHY CHOICE 10

HONOUR YOUR EMOTIONS

Your feelings are valid simply because they are yours. There is no need to apologise or explain – always be true to yourself. I find it helps to acknowledge that your emotions can be a compass for your life, offering clear guidance about how you are treating yourself and how your thoughts are affecting you.

Emotions are what we feel, not who we are. Too often we allow them to dictate the choices we make and how we experience life. Anger, guilt, shame, sadness, fear, anxiety and frustration create a negative space to live from. It is time to release yourself from the low vibrations that are limiting your life.

Be responsible. Learn to manage your feelings and understand what you are doing to cause them. We can all do better when we follow our hearts and detach from our thoughts. If you are a sensitive individual, you will feel deeply for yourself and others. Perhaps your emotions are the universe speaking to you through your body and mind. Be willing to tune into your feelings, let go of judgment and embrace them with kindness, as you would for a friend.

All of our thoughts, perceptions, memories and feelings influence every cell in our body, and can manifest as various health issues. Repressing our emotions will prevent the stream of life from flowing in a productive manner. Learn to recognise that your emotions offer an important inner guidance system, letting you know if you are living in an environment of biochemical health or distress.

Tears can free us from pent-up emotions and prepare our bodies for fruitful new beginnings. Do you ever allow yourself to cry? Tears are not a sign of weakness. When honoured, they can even make us stronger and deepen our sense of self-worth. A wise friend of mine once said, 'Without rain, there is no life. Without tears, there can be no healing.'

True healing does not take place until we surrender to our feelings. So, you may wish to embrace your emotions and allow the tears to flow. Crying is a healthy way to cleanse the soul of pain, grief, fear and longing. This offers us the chance to recharge our batteries and restore a sense of balance in our lives.

***

A FINAL NOTE FROM ME

Today's Guidance:

The world can be a scary place if you let it

Full of uncertainty and fear

Take back your power, own your life

Choose to live your truth

Allow what is in your heart to guide you

One step at a time, one choice at a time

Feel your way forward with ease and grace

Trust in yourself and your wisdom

Don't try to look too far ahead, or you will miss the

magic of NOW!

'YESTERDAY IS HISTORY. TOMORROW IS A MYSTERY.
TODAY IS A GIFT. THAT'S WHY WE CALL IT THE PRESENT.'

– ELEANOR ROOSEVELT

FURTHER READING

People, books and websites that have helped me, and you may wish to explore:

BOOKS

COELHO PAULO (1993) *The Alchemist*, (Harper Torch), (New York USA)

DISPENZA JOE (2017) *Becoming Supernatural*, (Hay House, Inc), (USA)

DYER WAYNE W (2007) *Change Your Thoughts – Change your Life*, (Hay House, Inc), (USA)

EMOTO MASARU (2004) *The Healing Power of Water*, (Hay House, Inc), (USA)

EVANS ANNIE (2010) *Live the Life you Long for*, (Allen & Unwin), (NSW Australia)

GILLESPIE DAVID (2008) *Sweet Poison*, (Penguin Australia), (Australia)

HOLMES LEE (2015) *Heal Your Gut*, (Murdoch Books), (NSW Australia)

JAMIESON SUSAN (2010) *Medical To Mystical*, (Findhorn Press), (Scotland UK)

KING SCOTT ALEXANDER (2003) *Animal Dreaming*, (Blue Angel Publishing), (Victoria Australia)

KRALIK JOHN (2011) *365 Thank Yous*, (Hachette Books), (New York USA)

MYSS CAROLINE (1996) *Anatomy of the Spirit*, (Harmony Books, Crown publishers), (New York USA)

RUIZ DON MIGUEL (1997) *The Four Agreements*, (Amber-Allen publishing, Inc), (California USA)

SCHUCMAN HELEN (1976) *A Course in Miracles*, (Foundation for Inner Peace), (New York USA)

SEGAL INNA (2007) *The Secret Language of your Body*, (Beyond Words), (Oregon USA)

TOLLE ECKHART (2005) *A New Earth*, (Penguin Random House), (USA)

VIZANT IYANLA (1998) *One Day My Soul Just Opened Up*, (Fireside), (New York USA)

WEBSITES

LEE CARROLL	https://kryon.com and kryonmasters.com
SANDRA CHAMPLAIN	https://wedontdie.com
AMANDA ELLIS	https://amandaellis.co.uk
PAM GREGORY (ASTROLOGER)	https://thenextstep.uk.com
DR ASHOK GUPTA	https://guptaprogram.com
LEE HARRIS	https://leeharrisenergy.com
MONIKA MURANYI	https://monikamuranyi.com https://kryon.com
SACRED SCRIBE ANGEL NUMBERS	https://sacredscribesangelnumbers.blogspot.com
DR TERRY WAHLS	https://terrywahls.com
TIM WHILD	https://timwhild.com
SARYON MICHAEL WHITE	https://saryon.com

ACKNOWLEDGEMENTS

To my husband Ian, my greatest supporter. Thank you for standing by me through all the tears, tantrums and sleepless nights. And for sharing my deep desire to help others in light of all we have learned. You always believe in me, even when I cannot! To my precious family: my son and daughter-in-law, daughter and son-in-law, and four unique and infinitely loveable grandchildren. You make the world a better place.

To my parents and parents-in-law (in spirit) for your unconditional love and support. I am thrilled that we have found ways to continue this journey together, and am grateful for your higher perspective. I know you have been beside me every step of the way.

To my team of editors and book designers: Leeza, Poppy and Ina. You have brought my dreams to reality and made a challenging journey worthwhile. I deeply appreciate your expertise and guidance. Thank you for keeping me (reluctantly) focused on the practical tasks of the final few months.

To everyone who has befriended me upon this long and winding road (too many beautiful souls to name). Thanks for your love and encouragement. And to all who have sought my counsel and trusted me to guide you. You have helped me to find my voice, hone my skills, and grow in self-belief.

Finally, to all who are facing a health or life challenge with courage and an open heart, I salute you. It may not be an easy path, but it will certainly be worth your effort. May you find many unexpected blessings along the way.

www.ingramcontent.com/pod-product-compliance
Lightning Source LLC
Chambersburg PA
CBHW050311010526
44107CB00055B/2195